THE KILLER ANGELS

Michael Shaara

TECHNICAL DIRECTOR Maxwell Krohn
EDITORIAL DIRECTOR Justin Kestler
MANAGING EDITOR Ben Florman

SERIES EDITORS Boomie Aglietti, Justin Kestler
PRODUCTION Christian Lorentzen, Camille Murphy

WRITER Catherine Buchanan
EDITORS Benjamin Morgan, Dennis Quinio, John Crowther

This edition published by Spark Publishing

Spark Publishing
A Division of SparkNotes LLC
120 Fifth Avenue, 8th Floor
New York, NY 10011

Any book purchased without a cover is stolen property, reported as "unsold and
destroyed" to the Publisher, who receives no payment for such "stripped books."

02 03 04 05 SN 9 8 7 6 5 4 3 2 1

Please send all comments and questions or report errors to
feedback@sparknotes.com.

Library of Congress information available upon request

Printed and bound in the United States

RRD-C

ISBN 1-58663-524-7

INTRODUCTION: STOPPING TO BUY SPARKNOTES ON A SNOWY EVENING

Whose words these are you *think* you know.
Your paper's due tomorrow, though;
We're glad to see you stopping here
To get some help before you go.

Lost your course? You'll find it here.
Face tests and essays without fear.
Between the words, good grades at stake:
Get great results throughout the year.

Once school bells caused your heart to quake
As teachers circled each mistake.
Use SparkNotes and no longer weep,
Ace every single test you take.

Yes, books are lovely, dark, and deep,
But only what you grasp you keep,
With hours to go before you sleep,
With hours to go before you sleep.

Contents

NOTE: This SparkNote uses the Ballantine edition of *The Killer Angels* published in 1974.

CONTEXT

MICHAEL SHAARA WAS BORN in 1928 in Jersey City, New Jersey. He made his name writing pulp science fiction in the 1950s. He later began writing mainstream fiction and was published in many magazines. During a visit to Gettysburg, Shaara saw the battlefield and learned about the battle and its significance. He returned home with the idea to write a historical novel based on the battle. Most historical novels use fictional characters in historical settings, but Shaara chose to write about the real-life participants in the battle, such as Robert E. Lee and Joshua L. Chamberlain. This unusual decision gives the novel a much more epic tone, but it also causes problems with historical accuracy. Because it uses real rather than invented characters, *The Killer Angels* is in many ways more similar to Shakespeare's historical plays in its style and tone than it is to other American historical novels, such as Stephen Crane's work about the Civil War, *The Red Badge of Courage*. Shaara died of a heart attack in 1988.

Published in 1974, *The Killer Angels* never enjoyed commercial success in Shaara's lifetime. But to the surprise of many, including Shaara, it won the 1975 Pulitzer Prize for Literature. Nevertheless, *The Killer Angels* remained a relatively obscure novel until it was adapted into the 1993 film *Gettysburg*, starring Martin Sheen and Jeff Daniels. With the release of the film, the novel shot to number one on the New York Times bestseller list. Since then, Shaara's son Jeff has written two more Civil War novels that detail the events preceding and following his father's book.

The Battle of Gettysburg, which the novel describes, was the bloodiest battle of the American Civil War, with over 50,000 casualties in the span of three days. Many historians have called it the high-water mark of the Confederacy, when General Robert E. Lee hurled the entire strength of his army at the Union forces in an attempt to end the war by destroying his enemy. Lee had invaded the enemy territory of Pennsylvania for the second time. The first invasion culminated in the Battle of Antietam in Sharpsburg, Maryland, the previous year. By invading, Lee put himself in a position to move toward Washington, D.C. and take the capital. If he succeeded, the Confederate States of America would likely win the war and gain the right to declare themselves an independent country. But due to a series of problems, the Confederates were forced to retreat from Gettysburg with terrible losses and never again would move into Union territory.

The battle has long held a great fascination for Civil War historians. Scholars agree that, with the heavy casualties and demoralizing defeat suffered by the South, the Battle of Gettysburg was the turning point of the war—a loss from which the Confederacy never fully recovered. But the Battle of Gettysburg also has other unique characteristics. It was one of only two major battles fought on Union soil. It involved a huge infantry charge, called Pickett's Charge, which ended in horrific losses. It was a major Union victory, which at the time was rare. Most important, it was a Union victory when such a victory was desperately needed. A Union loss at Gettysburg would have put the capital in jeopardy. Finally, when we consider the many memorable smaller struggles within the Battle of Gettysburg, such as the legendary fighting on Little Round Top and Pickett's Charge, it is clear why the Battle of Gettysburg has become the most famous of Civil War battles.

Shaara's innovation is to write his fictional novel from the perspective of the real-life generals and soldiers who were involved in the battle. The epic scope that this innovation allows him to achieve comes at the cost of historical accuracy, both in the film and in the novel. But with the success of the film and Jeff Shaara's other Civil War novels, *The Killer Angels* is now assured a permanent position in the American literary landscape.

NOTE ON HISTORICAL ACCURACY

As a novel that attempts to offer a more lifelike and liquid retelling of the Battle of Gettysburg, Michael Shaara's *The Killer Angels* portrays actual historical figures and the actual events in which they participated during the Civil War. While much of his characterization and novelistic interpretation is based on careful study of letters, documents, and historical texts, Shaara does take significant liberties in his portrayal of the characters and their inner thoughts and emotions. Because it is important to explore these characters and events from both literary and historical angles, this SparkNote draws on both the literary aspect of the novel and historical fact and credible opinion regarding the Battle of Gettysburg.

PLOT OVERVIEW

THE KILLER ANGELS tells the story of the Battle of Gettysburg. On July 1, 1863, the Army of Northern Virginia, or Confederate army, and the Army of the Potomac, or Union army, fought the largest battle of the American Civil War. When the battle ended, 51,000 men were dead, wounded, or missing. All the characters in the novel are based on real historical figures. They include General Robert E. Lee, commander of the Confederate army; General James Longstreet, Lee's second in command; and Union Colonel Joshua L. Chamberlain, who participated in one of the most famous segments of the Battle of Gettysburg, the fighting on Little Round Top.

The story begins on June 30, 1863. A spy comes to Longstreet and informs him that he has seen the Union army moving nearby. This information surprises Longstreet, because General J. E. B. Stuart is supposed to be tracking the Union army with his cavalry. Longstreet thinks the Confederate army must quickly move north to intercept the Union. The Confederates swing southeast through the mountains and toward a small town called Gettysburg.

Miles south of Gettysburg, Union Colonel Joshua L. Chamberlain awakes to discover that his regiment, the Twentieth Maine, has a hundred new members—mutineers from the Second Maine. Chamberlain gives them a brief speech, asking them to continue to fight, and all but six of the men join the Twentieth Maine freely.

In Gettysburg, General John Buford, leader of the Union cavalry, rides into the town and discovers Confederate troops nearby. He realizes that the two armies may end up fighting in the town, so he takes his two brigades—approximately 2,000 men—and positions the soldiers along the hills in the area. He knows that having high ground is the key to winning the battle, since it is easier to fight from above than below. In the Confederate camp, Longstreet meets with George Pickett and several other generals.

On the morning of July 1, Lee rises and curses Stuart's absence. He is blind without Stuart, because without him he has no idea where the Union army is. He meets with Longstreet, who wants to swing southeast and come between the Union army and Washington, D.C. Then, Longstreet says, the Confederates can use defensive tactics and have a much better chance of winning the battle. Lee refuses, because he wants to smash the Union army aggressively in one decisive stroke.

Meanwhile, the battle begins at Gettysburg when the Confederates attack Buford's men. Buford holds the Confederates off until infantry General John Reynolds arrives. Reynolds positions his troops and fights the Confederates off, but he is soon killed. Lee arrives in Gettysburg and finds the battle in full fury. Two other Confederate generals arrive and send word to Lee that they have engaged the Union troops, who continue to pour in from the south. Lee orders his generals to attack. Meanwhile, Chamberlain's regiment begins to move northward toward Gettysburg.

The first day's battle ends with the Union forces retreating into the hills surrounding Gettysburg. There they dig in, setting up cannons and defensive stone walls. Longstreet is nervous—he knows that the hills are good defensive positions, and he knows that Lee plans to attack them rather than swing the army southeast toward Washington, D.C. Lee meets with his generals and is angry with General Ewell for not following his orders and taking Cemetery Hill and Culp's Hill, thereby instead allowing the Union forces to retreat into them. Ewell is a cautious general, perhaps too cautious. Meanwhile, Buford returns to the Union camp to discover that he is being blamed for the day's loss.

On July 2, Chamberlain awakes and his regiment begins moving north again toward Gettysburg. On the way, his regiment discovers an escaped slave, and Chamberlain muses on the reasons behind the war and his thoughts on race. Back at Gettysburg, two of Lee's generals—Ewell and Early—suggest that the army strike the Union's two flanks in order to weaken it. Lee likes the plan, but Longstreet still wants to move southeast toward Washington, D.C. Lee refuses, and Longstreet reluctantly agrees to attack the Union's left flank. As he leads his troops toward the hills to the south of Gettysburg, Little Round Top and Big Round Top, he discovers that the army has come down off the hills and into the peach orchard at the bottom. He decides he has no choice but to attack anyway, and a bloodbath on both sides is the result.

Chamberlain's regiment finally reaches Gettysburg and is placed on Little Round Top. Chamberlain is told that he is the extreme left of the Union line, which means he can never retreat. Chamberlain and his men hold the hill against numerous Confederate attacks, but eventually they run out of bullets. Chamberlain orders a bayonet charge, and his screaming regiment, charging down the hill, frightens the Confederates into fleeing. The Union still controls Little Round Top at the end of the day, and Longstreet's men have suffered heavy losses in the peach orchard. That night, Stuart returns, and Lee scolds him for being absent. Lee then decides on a plan for the next day: now that he has battered the two flanks of the Union army, the middle must be weakened. He will charge through the middle of the Union line and split the army in two, then destroy each half individually.

The next morning, July 3, Chamberlain's men are moved to the center of the Union line, where it is supposed to be safe and quiet. At the Confederate camp, Longstreet tries to convince Lee one last time to swing the army toward Washington, D.C., but Lee again refuses. He is intent on attacking his enemy. Longstreet tells Lee that he is certain Lee's plan is doomed to failure, but Lee obstinately refuses to budge. Longstreet reluctantly agrees to attack the center of the line and places Pickett in charge of the assault.

The Confederates begin with an artillery barrage in an attempt to weaken the Union artillery on the other side. Chamberlain finds himself and his regiment in the middle of this bombardment, much to his surprise, but he survives intact. Since the Confederate artillery shoots too high, not much damage is dealt to the Union batteries. The Confederate attack begins as the troops start marching across the open field toward the Union troops. The Union begins firing cannons, blowing huge holes in the Confederate line and killing hundreds of men. When the Confederates come within range, the Union soldiers open fire with their guns, killing hundreds more. Pickett loses sixty percent of his division. The Confederates soon retreat, and the Battle of Gettysburg comes to its bloody, spectacular end.

Character List

General Robert E. Lee Confederacy. The Commander of the
Army of Northern Virginia, or Confederate army. At
the age of fifty-seven, Lee has become one of the most
famous—and most revered—men in the South. He has
led his army through a string of victories. At the time
of the Battle of Gettysburg, Lee is having heart
trouble, and he eventually dies of heart disease in
1870. In his foreword, Shaara writes that Lee is "a
man in control. He does not lose his temper nor his
faith. He believes absolutely in God. He loves Virginia
above all, the mystic dirt of home. He is the most
beloved man in either army."

General James Longstreet Confederacy. Lee's second in
command and, since the death of "Stonewall"
Jackson, his most important general. At forty-two,
Longstreet is full-bearded, slow talking, and crude. He
is aware of the new nature of warfare, and he knows
that military tactics have to change with new
technology. He is very stubborn, but he has great
respect for Robert E. Lee, and ultimately he defers to
his commander's judgment, though not without a good
deal of argument. All three of his children were killed
by a fever during the winter before the Battle of
Gettysburg. This loss has sunk the usually jovial
Longstreet into a depression that is severe at times.

Colonel Joshua Lawrence Chamberlain Union. Thirty-four
years old, Chamberlain has left his home in Maine and a
comfortable professorship at Bowdoin College to come
to war. He is the colonel of the Twentieth Maine Infantry
regiment. He was an excellent student at school, speaks
seven languages, and has a lovely singing voice, but all
his life he has wanted to be a soldier. He lied to Bowdoin
and told them he was going on sabbatical to France
because they would not let him go to war. He is an
intellectual, given to brooding and poetic thoughts.

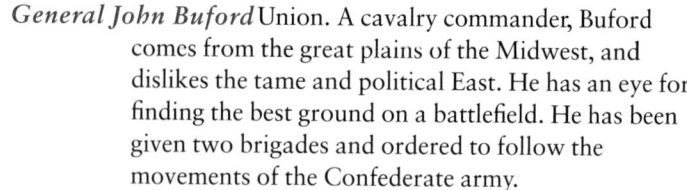

General John Buford Union. A cavalry commander, Buford comes from the great plains of the Midwest, and dislikes the tame and political East. He has an eye for finding the best ground on a battlefield. He has been given two brigades and ordered to follow the movements of the Confederate army.

Arthur Fremantle An Englishman sent to observe the Confederate army in action. Many people in the Confederacy hold out hope that England will come to their aid, since the South still bears many of the traditional aspects of English society, particularly in its class structure. But realists like Lee and Longstreet know that England will never help the Confederacy as long as it endorses slavery. Fremantle is tall and thin and reminds Longstreet of Ichabod Crane. Fremantle is dismayed by the rough manners of many of the soldiers, but he is also amazed at how much the Southerners are like Englishmen. He especially admires Robert E. Lee and James Longstreet. He is very enthusiastic about the battles, but he rarely has any idea of what is really going on.

General George Pickett Confederacy. Perfumed, with bouncing curly hair, George Pickett is a true dandy. Last in his class at West Point, Pickett has nonetheless risen to the rank of major general, and he leads an entire division. He is in love with a girl half his age and, in his typical melodramatic style, he has sworn to her that he would never drink. His division has not seen action in battle yet, and he longs for a chance to prove himself and his men.

General J. E. B. Stuart Confederacy. Stuart is the cavalry leader assigned by Lee to track the movements of the Union army. A fun-loving publicity hound, Stuart is off joyriding for the first two days of the battle, and it is his negligence that causes the Confederate army to lose track of the Union troops in the first place. Because of Stuart's absence, during the first two days the Confederates never know where the Union troops are or what the surrounding area looks like.

Thomas Chamberlain Union. Joshua's brother and aide, also in the Twentieth Maine. Not as smart or as brooding as his brother, Tom is more social, funnier, and more easygoing. While he has been a calming presence to his brother, he soon becomes a liability when Joshua Chamberlain realizes that he might, at some point, order his brother to his death.

General Lew Armistead Confederacy. At forty-six, Armistead is a widower, and his wife's death constantly causes him sorrow. A general serving in Pickett's division, Armistead knows that his old friend, Winfield Hancock, is on the other side of the war, serving as a general in the Union army. Armistead and Hancock will both be at the Battle of Gettysburg.

General Richard Ewell Confederacy. Recently chosen to replace part of "Stonewall" Jackson's command, Ewell has become unsure of himself after suffering an injury that cost him his leg. As Jackson's replacement, Ewell has a great amount of responsibility, which is a source of concern to Lee. Lee is particularly troubled by the way that Ewell defers to Jubal Early.

General Jubal Early Confederacy. A young, ambitious, and cold general. Like Ewell, he has been given a part of Jackson's old command. He accepts this responsibility easily. He is capable and confident, but also pushy, particularly with Ewell. Though Ewell technically has the greater responsibility and the greater control, he defers to Early. Longstreet and Armistead despise Early.

Private Buster Kilrain Union. A former sergeant who was demoted to private for drunkenly assaulting a fellow officer. A big, stocky Irishman, Kilrain is getting old and knows he does not have many fights left in him. He becomes a friend and mentor to his colonel, Joshua Chamberlain.

General John Reynolds Union. An intelligent infantry general who has a gift for positioning troops, Reynolds refuses to become the commander of the Union army, a position that is then given to George Meade. Reynolds is killed shortly after the action begins at Gettysburg.

General George Meade Union. Recently appointed commander of the Union armies, Meade arrives a bit late to the Battle of Gettysburg. Cautious but intelligent, he makes only a brief appearance in *The Killer Angels*.

Sorrel Confederate. An aide to Longstreet. Sorrel is a competent but not very sociable man.

General John Hood Confederate. A major general under Longstreet's command, Hood is Longstreet's most competent soldier. Like Longstreet, he prefers defensive strategies, and he understands that the nature of war is changing.

General Isaac Trimble Confederate. An old general who participates in Pickett's Charge.

General Winfield Scott Hancock Union. A competent, important general of the Union army, who directs much of the action at Gettysburg. He is an old friend of Confederate General Lew Armistead, who fights on the other side at Gettysburg.

General Ambrose Powell Hill Confederate. A general whose troops do much of the fighting on the first day of the battle, first with Union General John Buford's cavalry, then John Reynolds's infantry.

ANALYSIS OF MAJOR CHARACTERS

GENERAL ROBERT E. LEE

Robert E. Lee, the commander of the Confederate army, was one of the most beloved men in the American South, the darling of Virginia society. Lee is fifty-seven years old at the time of the Battle of Gettysburg, and has less than a decade to live. He is having heart trouble, which will one day kill him. Some historians have speculated that Lee may have suffered a mild heart attack during the Battle of Gettysburg, and Shaara works from that idea. Lee is a brilliant tactician, but his traditional ideas frequently conflict with the more visionary policies of Longstreet, a Confederate general who constantly advises a defensive position.

Shaara characterizes Lee as a wise old man, a brilliant commander who knows he is nearing the end of his career. Lee fervently holds on to the traditional ways of combat even while recognizing the importance of Longstreet's newer ideas. Lee inspires his troops—even as the wounded soldiers stagger back from Pickett's Charge, they beg him to let them attack again. Lee's presence alone helps keep Confederate morale high. But Lee's confidence in his army leads him to overestimate his men, causing the disaster of Pickett's Charge.

COLONEL JOSHUA L. CHAMBERLAIN

Chamberlain is the main Union voice in the novel. He provides a different view of the war than that of Lee or Longstreet, since as a colonel, he is significantly lower in rank than they. But Chamberlain is one of the most interesting Union soldiers of the Civil War, and certainly one of the most popular. Chamberlain led a fascinating life. He was a professor at Bowdoin College at the time of the war, left the college to fight, and distinguished himself as an excellent soldier by the end of the war. It was Chamberlain who accepted the surrender of the Confederate forces at Appomattox. The novel tries to strike a delicate balance between describing

Chamberlain as a college professor and as a soldier. Compared to many of his fellow soldiers, he is quite educated and thoughtful. For many, he is the easiest character with which to identify, since he is not only a citizen-turned-soldier, but is also lower ranked than the generals. Chamberlain is the idealized citizen-soldier, the man who chooses to forsake his comfortable job for his country and lives to become a renowned soldier.

Throughout the novel, Chamberlain constantly evaluates everything he sees, often poetically. He analyzes what he sees around him, and he has a much closer, more hands-on experience with the battle than many of Shaara's other characters. He is also in a difficult position because his brother, Tom, is one of his aides. Chamberlain realizes during the novel that he may be required to order Tom into harm's way, perhaps even to his death. Chamberlain is the soldier with the soul of a poet, and he provides the novel with some of its best and most insightful analysis of the feelings and motivations of Union soldiers during the Civil War.

GENERAL JAMES LONGSTREET

After the death of "Stonewall" Jackson, Longstreet becomes Lee's second in command. A stubborn man, depressed because of the recent death of his children, Longstreet enters the Battle of Gettysburg with high hopes of success, provided that Lee swings the Confederate army to the southeast and comes between the Union army and Washington, D.C. Longstreet knows that this strategy would make the Washington politicians force the Union commander, George Meade, to attack the Confederate army. If the Confederates dig into good ground, then they can simply destroy the Union army as it comes at them. The disagreement between Longstreet and Lee regarding this strategy, however, forms the main conflict between the two characters. Lee is continuously annoyed by Longstreet's stubbornness, and Longstreet is depressed by Lee's opposition to his defensive tactics.

Shaara portrays Longstreet as a man ahead of his time, someone who has seen the future of warfare and knows that it will be won through the proper use of technology. He envisions the fact that offensive warfare will become exceedingly difficult in the future. But this vision of Longstreet does not necessarily correspond to history. Longstreet became an advocate of defensive tactics after seeing how well they worked for the Confederate forces at the Battle of Fredericksburg—his belief in their efficacy did not come from some visionary understanding of the future of warfare. Longstreet had some advanced ideas, but few of them were put into effect, and those that were often failed. Lee's decision not to follow his general's advice was understandable as well: Lee had an impressive list of strategic victories prior to the Battle of Gettysburg. In this instance, Longstreet's suggestion probably would have worked well, but Longstreet had made suggestions in the past that had not worked. Also, Lee's strategies at Gettysburg were continually thwarted, sometimes by his own men. If Lee had with him at Gettysburg "Stonewall" Jackson, a man who understood Lee better than anyone else and knew how to move troops well, Lee's strategies might very well have worked. When considered in relation to history, Shaara's portrayal of Longstreet is decidedly too sympathetic. Longstreet takes little blame for the loss, when in fact his delays on the second and third days caused serious problems for the Confederate army's attack.

Themes, Motifs & Symbols

Themes

Themes are the fundamental and often universal ideas explored in a literary work.

Technology and Strategic Development

The Battle of Gettysburg is viewed by many historians as a turning point between the old methods of warfare and the new methods, changes that were dictated by the development of new technologies such as repeating rifles and long-range artillery. The Civil War saw the first ironclad battleships and the last great infantry charge: Pickett's Charge. The devastating losses of that charge—Pickett lost sixty percent of his division—marked the beginning of the end of the usefulness of infantry in major warfare. Cannons, grenades, tanks, planes, and missiles would eventually make infantry relatively obsolete.

Longstreet's continual insistence on defensive warfare and Lee's continual resistance to it best illustrates the conflict within the changing nature of warfare. Shaara portrays Lee as a traditional soldier of the Napoleonic mold: a brilliant strategist but an outdated one. Longstreet, by contrast, is portrayed as a grim realist who recognizes the changing nature of warfare and wants to change to match it. He knows that the Confederate army can never successfully invade the North. The Confederate army is smaller than the Union army and always will be, and the officers do not know the Northern lands as well as they do their native Virginia. Longstreet wants to hide behind stone walls and in trenches and cut down the enemy as it advances, while Lee prefers to strike out in the open, honorably, and simply overpower the enemy with good strategic maneuvering. But Lee's strategies are not as effective in a world using long-distance rifles and artillery.

The Obtrusiveness of Death in War

Although *The Killer Angels* reads like an adventure novel, it describes one of the bloodiest battles in the history of the Civil War. As he awaits the next battle, Chamberlain remembers piling up corpses at a previous battle to protect himself from bullets. He instinctively orders his brother to plug a hole in the regiment line and realizes he may have ordered his brother to his death. Limbs are sawed off wounded men to save them from infection, but Kilrain still dies from amputation and blood loss. During Pickett's Charge, soldiers are blown apart by artillery, "and here and there, tumbling over and over like a blood-spouting cartwheel, [was] a piece of a man."

This is a world where death can come at any time, and the men all have to learn to deal with that uncertainty. Chamberlain and his men are particularly vulnerable, since they are not generals protected in the rear of their lines. But everyone is forced to face death. Lee is dealing with heart trouble, which will eventually kill him—he knows he is an old man and has not long to live. Longstreet has lost three children that winter to fever, while Chamberlain is scarred by the memory of Fredericksburg. Just as the battle begins, General John Reynolds is killed instantly by a sniper. And General Lew Armistead marches across the entire field during Pickett's Charge only to be cut down at the end without ever meeting his friend Winfield Hancock. War novels may be read as adventure novels, but in real war there is death, and the hundreds of corpses that pile up over the course of *The Killer Angels* serve to remind us that Gettysburg was a real battle that left many men dead.

A Nation Divided

During the actual war the soldiers of the Confederacy and of the Union often tended to demonize one another. In order to be able to kill someone, the soldiers had to think of that person as less than human, or else the guilt could be unbearable. After the 1860s, the rise of Civil War nostalgia and Civil War enthusiasts gave the war a glossy, clean, glorified sheen. Both the North and the South are often presented as noble men fighting for their way of life—against slavery, or for federal control of states. But there are few examples of this demonization or hatred in *The Killer Angels*: it is a war between gentlemen. The lack of examination of these issues may be due to the fact that the novel focuses almost exclusively on men of the upper parts of society, particularly on the Confederate side: colonels and generals, never privates or sergeants.

As a character, Chamberlain illustrates the nation's division. Chamberlain ruminates several times on a discussion he had with a Southern professor, and it is evident that Chamberlain himself is divided: on the one hand, he holds the Northern abolitionist belief that blacks deserve to be free, but on the other hand, he is troubled by the sense of revulsion that he feels at the sight of a black man early in the novel. The professor initially argued with Chamberlain, saying that blacks are subhuman, and, of course, Chamberlain disagreed. However, when seeing the injured black man, Chamberlain notices what he thinks of as the man's animal-like qualities and wonders if the professor's purported subhuman view is plausible.

Chamberlain suffers from a form of internal division, but it is fairly clear that his cause is not the expressed cause of the Union. The Union's leaders, including Lincoln, never claimed to be fighting a war of liberation: they fought because they believed the Southern states were forbidden to secede. But Chamberlain fights for liberation, though most officers, such as Kilrain, do not. Kilrain, in fact, fights primarily to prove he is a brave man and perhaps also to bring down what he sees as overly aristocratic Southerners. But the most explicit symbol of this theme is the friendship between Lew Armistead and Winfield Hancock. Good friends that took different sides in the war, the two men participate in the same battle for the first and last time at Gettysburg. Throughout the novel, Armistead's sundered friendship with Hancock serves as a reminder of the hard lines that the Civil War drew between Americans.

MOTIFS

Motifs are recurring structures, contrasts, or literary devices that can help to develop and inform the text's major themes.

LOYALTY

Loyalty is essential for an army to function well, as soldiers have to trust their officers in order to follow them successfully. The idea of loyalty appears many times in *The Killer Angels*: Kilrain is loyal to Chamberlain; Goree and Sorrel are loyal aides to Longstreet; and most important, the entire Confederate army is fiercely loyal to Robert E. Lee.

But loyalty can be a double-edged sword, as Longstreet learns. Despite his absolute certainty that Pickett's Charge will fail and result in the death of thousands of men, he cannot bring himself to ask his fellow officers to turn against Lee. He knows that the other officers and the other soldiers would never follow him instead of Lee. But he cannot refuse to lead the charge himself because he is bound by his own loyalty to Lee and to Virginia—he is the best and only man for the job. Loyalty has helped bring about many of the Confederacy's victories, but at Gettysburg it contributes to the loss.

COMMAND ERRORS

Most of the primary characters in *The Killer Angels* are generals, or at least colonels. Each of these men is in command of a vast number of soldiers, and so each of their mistakes is magnified. The history of the Battle of Gettysburg consists of a series of tactical mistakes, and, in each case, the result is the death of hundreds, even thousands of men. For the Confederacy, the trouble begins early, when General J. E. B. Stuart, commander of the Confederate cavalry, fails to report promptly on the movements of the Union army. This absence prevents Lee from having accurate and timely information about the size and position of his enemy, and it allows the Union an unexpected element of surprise. The next mistake is Generals Ewell and Early's failure to take the high ground when they have the chance. This mistake is partially Lee's fault as well, since he does not make it clear how necessary it is to take the hill. The results are ultimately disastrous: without the high ground, the Confederacy must fight a losing battle when it chooses to attack. Later, Longstreet again has inaccurate knowledge of the Union position, and he is forced to lose hours of time by countermarching his troops to another position. Of course, the greatest failure is Pickett's Charge, which, in hindsight, was one of the worst tactical decisions of the Civil War. The charge cost thousands of lives and, in the opinion of many historians, broke the back of the Confederate war effort.

ARISTOCRACY

Since much of the book is written from the perspective of the Confederate leaders, we are given a close look into the high society of the Old South. Lee and Pickett in particular are examples of the "Southern gentleman," and represent values that they believe would be erased by a Union victory. Historically, the Union army was much more ethnically diverse than the Confederate army, being filled with immigrants and the children of immigrants. While the Union commanders were primarily white Anglo-Saxons, they were not necessarily rich white men. The Southern commanders, on the other hand, were primarily rich white men of British ancestry, with a few exceptions such as Longstreet, who was not as wealthy and was part Dutch. In *The Killer Angels*, this motif manifests itself in a few ways. For Buster Kilrain, the war is less about freeing slaves than it is about leveling the social playing field: "The point is that we have a country here where the past cannot keep a good man in chains, and that's the nature of the war. It's the aristocracy I'm after. 'All that lovely, plumed, stinking chivalry. The people who look at you like a piece of filth, a cockroach, ah.'" On the other side, Arthur Fremantle, the British observer, can think of nothing better than seeing the Confederacy win and preserve the class system inherited from the Old World—to him, the point is that the people of the South "do it all exactly as we do in Europe. And the North does not. That's what the war is really about. . . . The Northerner doesn't give a damn for tradition, or breeding, or the Old Country. . . . Of course, the South is the Old Country. They haven't left Europe. They've merely transplanted it. And that's what the war is about."

Symbols

Symbols are objects, characters, figures, or colors used to represent abstract ideas or concepts.

Lee's Heart Trouble

There is historical evidence that Robert E. Lee may have suffered from heart trouble during the Battle of Gettysburg and that he may even have had a mild heart attack. Shaara uses this fact to develop a minor, but powerful theme: Lee's heart has been broken by the war. Longstreet at one point reminds Lee that when they became officers in the United States army, they swore to defend all of the United States. They have even led many of the Union soldiers. Now, they are killing them. Lee has been forced to choose between his beloved Virginia and his country, and to him that is no real choice: his first duty is always to Virginia. But the decision has left him heartbroken, and as the war drags on his heartbreak only becomes worse. At one point in the novel, Lee tells Longstreet that the true sadness of the career soldier is the obligation to order men to their deaths. The war has taken a heavy toll on Lee, both physically and mentally, and both are a part of the pain Lee constantly feels in his chest.

SUMMARY & ANALYSIS

INTRODUCTION AND FOREWORD

SUMMARY—INTRODUCTION AND FOREWORD

In the opening section, "To the Reader," author Michael Shaara states that he wrote the book because he wanted to know "what it was like to be there, what the weather was like, what the men's faces looked like." He adds that since there were so many different historical interpretations of what went on at the Battle of Gettysburg, he based *The Killer Angels* primarily on the letters, journal entries, and memoirs of the men who were there.

In the Foreword, Shaara gives a brief description of the situation in late June 1863. General Robert E. Lee, after a string of victories, has led the Confederate army into an invasion of Union territory, mainly in Pennsylvania. His intention is to destroy the Union army once and for all and then offer peace to the President of the Union, Abraham Lincoln—with the understanding that the Confederacy be recognized as an independent country.

Shaara then describes the main characters and gives a little of each man's background and personal history. The most important are General Robert E. Lee, Confederate General James Longstreet, Union Colonel Joshua Lawrence Chamberlain, and Major General George Meade, commanding general of the Union army.

ANALYSIS—INTRODUCTION AND FOREWORD

In "To the Reader," Shaara says that his desire to understand the war from the perspective of someone who participated in it is the same as that of Stephen Crane, the author of another famous Civil War novel, *The Red Badge of Courage*. Crane's novel, written only a decade or so after the Civil War, is an important precursor to *The Killer Angels*, since it was the first fictionalization of the war.

Shaara's list of characters provides some necessary information about the key players, but the character traits and background history we are given here are also included in the novel itself. Some of the novel's perspectives and biases are hinted at here. For instance,

Shaara introduces nine Confederate characters, but only five Union characters. In fact, with the exception of a few early chapters about John Buford, Joshua Chamberlain is the only Union voice we encounter in the novel. By contrast, there are chapters centering around five different Confederate characters, including a spy and a military observer from England who is visiting the Confederates, and the novel contains many more chapters from the viewpoint of the Confederates than it does from the Unionists.

JUNE 30, 1863: CHAPTERS 1–2

SUMMARY—CHAPTER 1: THE SPY

Daytime, Taneytown, Pennsylvania, a town near Gettysburg. Harrison, a Confederate spy, discovers a large mass of Union troops moving north. The Union troops are moving dangerously close to the Confederate army. Harrison returns in the middle of the night to the Confederate camp and reports his discovery to General James Longstreet. Longstreet is skeptical at first, but Harrison convinces him that he has actually seen the Union troops. Longstreet quickly wakes up General Robert E. Lee, commander of the Confederate army. Lee is also skeptical, since he has sent General J. E. B. Stuart out with his cavalry to keep an eye on the movements of the Union army. But Longstreet believes that Stuart is out joyriding. Longstreet presses Lee to get the army moving west. Lee agrees, deciding to move toward a town called Gettysburg.

SUMMARY—CHAPTER 2: CHAMBERLAIN

Daytime, several miles south of Gettysburg. Union Colonel Joshua L. Chamberlain is awakened by Buster Kilrain, a former sergeant who was demoted to private after assaulting another officer. Kilrain informs him that their regiment, the Twentieth Maine, has just received 120 men from the Second Maine, which has been disbanded. The new men are mutineers, having expected to be sent home after the disbanding of their regiment. The men are now being kept under guard, and Chamberlain has orders to shoot any man who does not agree to march. Chamberlain is joined by his younger brother, Tom, also a member of the Twentieth Maine. Chamberlain obtains food for the mutineers, then meets with their leader. The leader tells him that the mutineers are tired of the war and the inept Union generals who have been running it, and they want to go home. Chamberlain knows he cannot let them go, but he also cannot bring himself to shoot them. He tells them his predicament, then gives a stirring speech in which he asks them to join the Twentieth Maine. All but six men agree.

Analysis—June 30, 1863: Chapters 1–2

Michael Shaara has a difficult task in front of him as the novel begins. *The Killer Angels* is generally referred to as a "historical novel," but most historical novels are simply set in a certain time period and do not deal directly with the actions of people who really existed. For instance, Stephen Crane's classic Civil War novel, *The Red Badge of Courage,* follows a fictional soldier through several battles. *The Killer Angels* is more similar to the historical plays of William Shakespeare—Shaara gives a dramatized account of history, using characters and events drawn from real life. As such, parts of the book, especially the dialogue and the thoughts of the characters, are Shaara's creation, not based on documented history. Shaara based his characterizations primarily on the letters and memoirs of the soldiers and officers involved in the battle, but there is no way of knowing exactly what these officers really thought or said.

These two chapters introduce three of the book's most important characters: Lee, Longstreet, and Chamberlain. The Confederate point of view swings back and forth from Lee to Longstreet. Lee is an old man, a gentleman and a classic soldier of an earlier era who is brilliant in the type of tactics he was taught. Longstreet is something of a visionary, a man who is very aware of the changing nature of war as machines and defensive warfare become more important. Their differing perceptions of the nature of war form the backbone of the difficult relationship between these two men. Longstreet adores his commander, and he finds it difficult to argue with him. Ultimately, Longstreet always backs down in an argument with Lee, because he knows that he could never have the support of the army the way Lee does. But Longstreet is stubborn, and he constantly tries to convince Lee to fight defensively, encouraging Lee to move his troops to a different battlefield rather than fight the Union army on terrain that puts the Confederacy at a disadvantage.

Colonel Joshua L. Chamberlain is practically the only Union voice in the novel. Chamberlain is not a general, as are most of the major characters on the Confederate side. He is only a colonel, the leader of a regiment. There are a number of reasons that the novel follows Chamberlain's point of view when presenting the Union side. In the years following the Civil War, it became more and more apparent that the war had been decided at Gettysburg. It was the high point of the Confederacy, when the Confederate army, flushed with success, actually invaded Union territory. If Lee had been successful in destroying the Union army or capturing Washington, D.C., the North would have had to admit defeat, and the Confederacy would have been established as a new country. But the Union won the Battle of Gettysburg, and the battle itself was largely determined by the Battle of Little Round Top. Holding the extreme left flank of the army, Chamberlain led his regiment, which had run out of ammunition, down the hillside in a bayonet charge against the Confederate forces. The charge succeeded in repelling the Confederates, and Little Round Top was saved. As the years went by, the fighting on Little Round Top became more and more legendary, and by choosing to center on Chamberlain, Shaara focuses on one of the most popular characters of the battle.

Furthermore, the real Chamberlain led a fascinating life. He was a professor at Bowdoin College at the time of the war, left the college to fight, and distinguished himself as an excellent soldier by the end of the war. It was Chamberlain who accepted the surrender of the Confederate forces at Appomattox. Chapter 2 establishes the contrast between Chamberlain the college professor and Chamberlain the soldier. He is an unusually educated and thoughtful man compared with many other soldiers. For many, he is the easiest character with whom to identify, since he is not only a citizen-turned-soldier, but also only a colonel, not a higher-ranked commander or general like the other principal characters. In contrast, Lee and Longstreet represent heroic, almost mythical figures. Chamberlain, while also a source of nostalgic glory, is still a common citizen thrown into war.

June 30, 1863: Chapters 3–4

Summary—Chapter 3: Buford

Daytime, Gettysburg. General John Buford, commander of the Union cavalry, enters Gettysburg with his two brigades: 2,500 men, all mounted on horses. Buford is scouting the land ahead of the Union army. He spots a brigade of Confederate infantry in the town, and he is surprised to see them apparently without cavalry. He decides to remain in Gettysburg and sends a message back to the infantry commander, General John Reynolds, telling him that he has occupied Gettysburg and expects an even larger Confederate force to arrive the next morning.

Buford surveys the area around the town and notices its "high ground." Buford rides through the middle of the town with his men. The townspeople are relieved to see Union troops.

Buford decides to occupy the hills with his men. They dismount and get ready to fight on foot. He hopes to prevent the Confederates from taking the high ground the next day until Reynolds arrives with his troops.

SUMMARY — CHAPTER 4: LONGSTREET

Nighttime, Confederate camp west of Gettysburg. The Confederate officers try to teach Lieutenant Arthur Fremantle, a British military observer, how to play poker. Longstreet muses on the upcoming battle. One of his aides, Sorrel, informs Longstreet that a soldier spotted Union cavalry in Gettysburg. The reporting officer's commander, General Hill, thinks he must have seen a state militia, but Longstreet is not sure.

Longstreet continues to brood, chatting briefly with Fremantle. General George Pickett, a good soldier and a perfumed dandy, arrives, much to everyone's pleasure. Other officers under Pickett's command also arrive: Lew "Lo" Armistead, Jim Kemper, and Dick Garnett.

Pickett's division has not had much action. Now, the division has been placed at the rear of the army. Pickett approaches Longstreet and asks that his division be moved up, but Longstreet refuses, adding that if the army has to turn and run, Pickett's division will then be leading the fight to escape. Pickett leaves and Longstreet then talks to Armistead. Armistead's old friend, General Winfield Hancock, is in the Union army, and Longstreet speculates that he may soon meet his friend—in battle. Longstreet tells Armistead that he would prefer to use defensive warfare tactics, such as trenches. Armistead replies that his ideas are sound, but that the Confederate army is not the army to try them out on. Besides, Armistead says, General Lee would never agree to defensive warfare, because he thinks it is somewhat dishonorable.

Back at the poker game, several of the players, including a Southern politician, become upset at Fremantle for saying that the war is over slavery.

The next morning, skirmishes begin between Buford's men and the Confederate infantry in Gettysburg.

ANALYSIS — JUNE 30, 1863: CHAPTERS 3–4

The most important event in Chapter 3 is Buford's decision to try and hold the "high ground." The high ground consists of four hills: Culp's Hill, Cemetery Hill, Little Round Top, and Round Top. The hills are all connected by a long, crescent-shaped ridge called Cemetery Ridge. This high ground will be important throughout the entire novel. Control of the high ground gives an army several things: a good view of the entire battlefield; an excellent place from which to fire off artillery, meaning cannons; and a good defensive position. It is much more difficult to run uphill toward an enemy than it is to fire downhill at one. Little Round Top, in particular, has a lot of rocks that give good coverage against bullets and is so bare that it affords a view of several miles around. Civil War historians generally agree that the high ground was critical in the Battle of Gettysburg, and, therefore, Buford made an excellent move in realizing that fact and protecting it.

The chapter also reveals the difficult decisions a soldier must make, especially in the absence of his superior officers. Buford is unsure whether the Confederates are really coming, and he is particularly worried that if he decides to try and stop the Confederates from taking the hill, General Reynolds will not arrive in time to save Buford's brigades from heavy casualties and help keep the Confederates off the hills.

By switching the narrative point of view between the story's characters, Shaara is able to show how differently the various participants perceived the battle. Shaara establishes a pattern of choosing a single person on which to focus in each chapter, giving us only that person's perspective on the situation. This kind of narration is known as third-person subjective. This is different from an omniscient narrator, who can dive into the thoughts of any character and can make comments and judgments external to the story. For instance, in Chapter 3, an omniscient narrator might tell us what Buford's aide is thinking or comment in his own voice on how clever it was for Buford to secure the high ground. On the other hand, a subjective narrator never leaves the point of view of the character on which he is focused: we never read the thoughts of Buford's aide, we only read Buford's own thoughts. A subjective narrator does not interrupt the narration to make aside comments: the narrator might tell us what Buford's personality or mood was like, but he would not remark on the importance of Buford's decision to grab the high ground.

Also, this use of third-person subjective narration creates a sense of suspense in a story whose outcome we already know. Shaara's use of this form of third-person subjective narration means we are not always getting all the information about what is happening. Buford only knows his own thoughts: he does not know what General Reynolds is doing at any given moment, and he does not know what his aide is thinking unless he asks him. This style gives a very realistic portrayal of what events might have looked like to a participant, and in a novel that uses real-life historical characters, it is important for Shaara to make the characters seem as realistic as possible. People have been reading about Robert E. Lee, James Longstreet, and Joshua Chamberlain for more than a century. If Shaara wrote in the third-person omniscient point of view, the novel might have read like a very detailed history textbook. By using the subjective narration, Shaara draws us much deeper into the intricacies of characterization and mood, as opposed to merely the plot summary of the Gettysburg story.

Chapter 4 is an excellent example of this technique of limited perspective. It is a long chapter that serves primarily to introduce the moody, intelligent Longstreet, who has recently lost three children and no longer socializes with his troops. The chapter also introduces nearly a dozen other characters, such as the pompous English lieutenant, Arthur Fremantle, and the dandy General Pickett. Fremantle serves primarily to reinforce the long-held romantic notion that the predominantly Anglo-Saxon Confederate officers were true gentlemen who passed their wealth on from generation to generation, in the tradition of British high society. In contrast, the Northern officers came from many different ethnic backgrounds and from a society in which anyone who earned enough money could become rich and a member of the social elite.

JULY 1, 1863: CHAPTERS 1–2

SUMMARY — CHAPTER 1: LEE

Morning, Confederate camp west of Gettysburg. General Robert E. Lee rises. He is having some slight heart troubles and is taking things easy. He discusses the military situation with his aide, Taylor, noting that General Stuart has not reported back with the position of the Union army, thus leaving Lee blind. Several of Lee's officers want Stuart to be court-martialed for his failure to report on the Union army, but Lee is fond of Stuart, who has been an excellent soldier until now. Lee tells General Longstreet that he is Lee's most valuable officer and must not risk himself near the front in battle. Longstreet reports that the new commander of the Union army is George Meade. Longstreet adds that he believes Union cavalry have occupied Gettysburg. He suggests that the Confederate army swing around to the southeast of Gettysburg and put itself between the Union army and Washington, D.C., cutting the Union soldiers off from the capital and forcing them to attack. Lee is annoyed by Longstreet's stubborn advocacy of defensive tactics and refuses to use them. As the two ride out to start the day's march, they hear the sound of artillery fire in the distance.

SUMMARY — CHAPTER 2: BUFORD

Morning, Gettysburg. Confederate forces begin to attack General Buford's cavalry. Buford leads his men on foot, like infantry. After the initial Confederate attack, Buford sends word of the attack to General Reynolds, who is heading toward Gettysburg with his infantry troop. Buford fervently hopes that Reynolds arrives at Gettysburg before it is too late—Buford has lost battles before while waiting for infantry to arrive. Buford orders his cannoneers to fire several shots. The Confederate infantry attack begins. Buford rides back and forth among his soldiers, directing the battle. The Confederates outnumber the Union soldiers, but the Confederates have been expecting a small militia, and their early attacks are easily repulsed by Buford's men. Soon, however, the Confederates are attacking in droves, and the tide begins to turn. When Buford thinks he can hold out no more, Reynolds arrives and provides needed relief for Buford's brigade. Just as Reynolds's men move in, Reynolds is shot and killed. The attack continues without a commander, and Buford rides out to scout the other hills and make sure no Confederate forces are moving in on them.

ANALYSIS—JULY 1, 1863: CHAPTERS 1–2

Robert E. Lee is one of the most famous figures in the Civil War. A beloved general and the darling of Virginia society, Lee is fifty-seven years old at the time of the battle, and has less than a decade to live. He is having heart trouble, which eventually kills him. Some historians speculate that Lee may have suffered a mild heart attack during the Battle of Gettysburg, and Shaara works from that idea. This chapter also introduces the dynamic between Lee and Longstreet that will occupy much of their interaction: Longstreet fervently tries to persuade Lee to use defensive tactics against the Union army, and Lee constantly refuses to do so.

The Killer Angels probes the boundary between history and fiction. Shaara does not differentiate between what is factual in his writing and what is historical. The point of his novel is not to give a history of the Battle of Gettysburg. Rather, the novel is imaginative: it speculates on what it might have been like to participate in the battle and what the generals might have been thinking and feeling as it proceeded. Nonetheless, Shaara's work is carefully researched and is usually faithful to the events of the war. Shaara's attitudes toward his characters reflect his own interpretations of the historical figures. Longstreet emerges as one of Shaara's most developed characters in the book. Shaara is very sympathetic to the idea of a visionary Longstreet who understands the nature of "modern warfare" and is years ahead of his time in tactics.

Historians—particularly D. Scott Hartwig in *A Killer Angels Companion*—have argued that this depiction of Longstreet is debatable, since Longstreet "offered no imaginative or dramatic changes in tactics during the war," and only became an advocate for defensive tactics after watching the Confederate troops crush the Union troops at Fredericksburg by hiding behind stone walls and in trenches. Hartwig claims that Lee knew just as well as Longstreet how to fight the Civil War using modern weaponry. While a defensive posture might have worked for Lee at the Battle of Gettysburg, it is by no means certain that it would have, and Shaara's portrayal of Longstreet as a man ahead of his time is not necessarily accurate.

The developing dynamic between Longstreet and Lee suggests that their relationship is similar to that between a father and a son. Even though Lee is only eleven years older, Longstreet treats his commander with great respect and, when Lee is in pain or fails, with great sympathy. Ultimately, no matter how much he might disagree,

Longstreet defers to Lee's decisions. Shaara, like many historians, places the blame for the Confederate defeat at Gettysburg squarely on Lee's shoulders, as Lee himself does. In the process, Shaara removes much of the blame that Longstreet should have shouldered, making Lee's failure that much more tragic: the great, legendary General Lee, the brilliant tactician, fails to win a battle that his best general could have won for him. Longstreet's defensive tactics would not necessarily have worked, and Lee's tactical decisions were not certain to fail. Some historians, like Hartwig, argue that many of Lee's tactics were quite sound.

The battle actually begins in Chapter 2 when the Confederates attack Buford's two cavalry brigades, who have dismounted and are fighting on foot. Buford's troops are to the west of Gettysburg, blocking all the hills, including Seminary Ridge. Here, history provides Shaara with some high drama: General Reynolds was indeed killed by a sniper almost immediately after arriving with his men in Gettysburg. The loss of Reynolds robbed the Union forces of one of their best officers. Fortunately, Reynolds had ordered his troops into position before being shot, and the Union forces succeeded in preventing the Confederates from capturing the high ground.

JULY 1, 1863: CHAPTERS 3–4

SUMMARY — CHAPTER 3: LEE

Of course, I do not know his situation, and I do not want him to engage a superior force, but I do want him to take that hill, if he thinks practicable.
(See QUOTATIONS, p. 57)

Morning, Gettysburg. Lee arrives in Gettysburg to discover a small battle in full fury. General Heth's troops are engaged in battle against the Union infantry that has arrived to relieve Buford. Lee is annoyed because he has no information from General Stuart, the cavalry leader who has been assigned to report on the movements of the Union army. No one knows where Stuart is, and Longstreet thinks he is out joyriding. Lee surveys the field with binoculars and sees that Heth's forces have been forced back by the Union troops. Heth appears and tells Lee the story: he moved in to Gettysburg, thinking he would be fighting a militia, and discovered he was fighting Buford's dismounted cavalry. The cavalry put up a good fight, and just as Heth thought he might win, Union infantry—Reynolds's men—appeared and repulsed the attack.

As Heth tells this story, Lee receives reports from one of his generals, General Rodes, who informs him that his division has arrived along the northern flank of the Union army and has already engaged the enemy. He also sends word that Jubal Early's division will be joining his attack within an hour. It seems to Lee that everything is happening almost as if it were planned, and he tells Heth to attack again, along with General Pender's division. The battle rages, and then General Hill reports that Heth has been wounded and that the Union forces are fighting better than he remembers them ever doing. Eventually, the Confederate army forces the Union army back, and the Union troops fall back to the hills on the northern end of Cemetery Ridge, Cemetery Hill, and Culp's Hill. Lee sends a message to General Ewell, telling him to pursue the Union troops and to take the hill "if possible."

Longstreet arrives and surveys the scene. He suggests that the Confederate army should swing around behind the hills and position itself between the Union army and Washington, D.C. But Lee refuses to disengage—essentially to retreat and move the army—in the face of the enemy. A message arrives from Ewell—he has not yet taken Cemetery Hill because he fears a Union attack from the south of Gettysburg. Ewell never begins the attack, much to Lee's consternation.

Summary—Chapter 4: Chamberlain

> *Piled-up bodies in front of you to catch the bullets,*
> *using the dead for a shield; remember the sound?*
> (See QUOTATIONS, p. 58)

Afternoon, south of Gettysburg. Colonel Joshua L. Chamberlain marches his men toward Gettysburg. Tom, Chamberlain's brother, explains the personalized brigade bugle call to a new recruit. As he rides his horse, Chamberlain broods and daydreams, realizing that he is starting to love the life of the soldier. But he also recalls piling corpses to block bullets and the constant awareness in battle that one can die at any instant. He wonders if he has grown to love that too.

He then remembers his boyhood home, reciting the "What a piece of work is man!" speech from Shakespeare's Hamlet, which includes the line, "[I]n action, how like an angel!" He recalls how his father replied, "Well, boy, if he's an angel, he's sure a murderin' angel." The young Chamberlain then gave a class speech entitled "Man, the Killer Angel."

The regiment marches through the town of Hanover, whose residents are very glad to see Union troops. As they near Gettysburg, the soldiers receive word of the battle that day, and the regiment swiftly moves toward the town. They set up camp just outside the town and wait for morning.

ANALYSIS — JULY 1, 1863: CHAPTERS 3–4

Chapter 3 contains most of the major combat on the first day of the Battle of Gettysburg. The struggle is primarily between two of the five Union infantry divisions brought up by Reynolds and the divisions led by Heth, Rodes, and Early. The battle is something of a Confederate victory since the Confederates force the Union army back to Cemetery Ridge. But the Union troops start "digging in" to the hills, fortifying their positions behind stone walls and among trees and placing artillery on high ground. The Union forces are now facing west, toward Seminary Ridge, which runs parallel to Cemetery Ridge. From north (right) to south (left), the Union line starts at Culp's Hill and continues along Cemetery Ridge through Cemetery Hill down to Little Round Top. Culp's Hill lies to the east of Cemetery Hill, making the Union army's line curve. The shape of the Union line has often been compared to a fishhook with its barb at Culp's Hill, and its shank extending between Cemetery Hill and Little Round Top. This geography is important because Chamberlain's forces will occupy the southern side of Little Round Top, which means they are the extreme left flank of the Union army.

This chapter also contains one of the most infamous events in Civil War history. Lee orders Ewell to take Cemetery Hill if possible. Many historians have claimed that the hill would have been taken if Lee had given the same order to "Stonewall" Jackson, his right-hand man who was killed before the Battle of Gettysburg and replaced by Ewell and A.P. Hill. But Ewell—cautious, nervous, new to command, and still recovering from the loss of a leg—never attacks. Overnight, the Union forces dig in and fortify their positions, and Union reinforcements arrive, making the Confederates' attack much more difficult the next day. Many historians have blamed Ewell for losing Gettysburg because he did not take Culp's Hill on the first day before the Union reinforcements arrived. Other historians have blamed Lee for not appreciating the differences between Ewell and Jackson and therefore making his orders more explicit. Wherever the blame rests, the failure of the Confederacy to gain the high ground is often given as the reason that they lost the battle.

Stylistically, Chapter 4 is very different from the chapters that precede it, since there is almost no action and no plot. Chamberlain marches his men north toward Gettysburg and broods. After Longstreet, Chamberlain is the most developed character in the novel. Shaara characterizes Chamberlain as the quintessential citizen-turned-soldier, the Maine professor who suddenly finds himself piling up the corpses of fellow soldiers in order to shield himself from bullets. Chamberlain becomes very morbid as he recalls these actions and the sound of "the flap of a torn curtain in a blasted window, fragment-whispering in that awful breeze: never, forever, never, forever." Chamberlain chides himself for these thoughts and for his "professor's mind." Shaara uses Chamberlain to provide the thinking man's view of the Civil War. Lee and Longstreet are career soldiers—they have known only the army, and while they are educated gentlemen, they are not professors. Chamberlain, the intelligent man who left his comfortable life to come to war, has the clearest view of both sides of the conflict—the military as well as the civilian perspectives.

Chamberlain's chapters also give the best view of the everyday life of soldiers. Generals like Lee, Longstreet, and Buford eat well, play poker, and drink all the liquor they want. Chamberlain is only a colonel and his friends all serve under him, including his brother. Chamberlain's lower rank also means he has to deal with concerns such as arranging to handle men who faint from heat exhaustion and ensuring that the marching speed is maintained. Later, Chamberlain's chapters provide the only real description of combat from inside the battle itself.

JULY 1, 1863: CHAPTERS 5–6

SUMMARY—CHAPTER 5: LONGSTREET

Evening, Confederate camp just west of Gettysburg. Longstreet rides aimlessly on his horse and broods, examining the battlefield. He is anxious about the hills, because he recognizes the strategic importance of the high ground. Longstreet knows that Lee will attack the next day. Lee is "fixed and unturnable, a runaway horse," and Longstreet believes that Lee is making a mistake. But Lee will not listen to Longstreet, and Lee's reticence makes Longstreet depressed. Longstreet starts to think about his children, all three of them dead from fever over the winter, and he becomes even more depressed. He knows that the army is all that he has left.

Fremantle, the British observer, fumbles his way next to Longstreet. Fremantle is giddy with pleasure at having seen the fighting earlier that day. He is impressed by the Southern people, since they often seem similar to the English. He says that Lee is an English general, and that Lee has gained a reputation in Europe—mostly because Americans are never thought of as gentlemen. Fremantle adds, "You cannot imagine the surprise. One hears all these stories of Indians and massacres and lean backwoodsmen with ten-foot rifles and rain dances and what not, and yet here, your officers. . . . Why, do you know, your General Lee is even a member of the Church of England?" Fremantle hopes that the English and the Confederacy can become allies. England, however, never enters the war against the Union because the Confederates support slavery, to which England is opposed.

Fremantle and Longstreet also discuss "Stonewall" Jackson, Lee's former right-hand general who was killed before the Battle of Gettysburg. Another Confederate officer, Dick Garnett, was shamed when Jackson accused him of cowardice in retreating from an impossible fight, and Jackson tried to have Garnett court-martialed. Garnett, who now serves under General Pickett, had no chance to clear his name before Jackson died, and now he is depressed because of his dishonored reputation. "Honor without intelligence . . . could lose the war," Longstreet says, referring obliquely to Lee and his style of gentlemen's warfare. Longstreet describes how he believes a new form of fighting should be introduced, one that takes advantage of new weapon technology such as repeating rifles. But Lee, Longstreet thinks, "would rather lose the war than his dignity."

SUMMARY—CHAPTER 6: LEE

Lee meets with generals Ewell, Early, and Rodes. Lee wants to know why Ewell has not taken Cemetery Hill. Ewell claims that he did not think it possible. Early adds that there were rumors of Union forces to the north that had to be confirmed before they could make an attack, so they decided to wait for another general, Johnson, to arrive with his forces. Early adds that Cemetery Hill "will be a very strong position" for the Union forces.

Annoyed, but ready to move on, Lee asks Ewell if he can attack the right (northern) flank of the Union army the next day. Early thinks it would be a difficult fight, but if Longstreet attacks the left flank, it might draw enough Union troops to the south to make an attack by Ewell and Early worthwhile. Lee mentions Longstreet's suggestion that they move the army southeast and come between the Union army and Washington, D.C. Ewell thinks that to leave the town, which they have captured, would demoralize the troops, and Early thinks it unwise to move an entire army around the high, fortified position that the Union forces are holding. Privately, to himself, Lee agrees that it would be extremely difficult to move the army without Stuart and his cavalry to guide them.

Lee leaves and meets General Isaac Trimble, who is furious with Ewell for not having taken Cemetery Hill. Trimble tells Lee that he offered to take the hill with no more than a regiment, but Ewell made no response: he simply froze. Lee retires to his headquarters in an old house and considers his options. Lee sends for Ewell. Ewell arrives, somewhat sheepish, and tells his commander that he and Early think they should attack the right flank, as Lee suggested. Ewell apologizes for being too "careful" that day, and Lee, a gentleman, accepts the apology and does not chide Ewell very much. Lee goes to sleep, wondering where Stuart is.

ANALYSIS—JULY 1, 1863: CHAPTERS 5–6

Shaara decides to focus his novel on the Confederacy's view of the Battle of Gettysburg for several reasons. The battle is often referred to as the "high tide of the Confederacy," because it was as close as the Confederate States of America ever came to achieving their independence. They had invaded Northern territory and were now attempting to destroy the Union army once and for all. Lee knows that if they successfully destroy the Union army, the war will be over. This desire to completely vanquish his opponents may be part of the reason why Lee is so intent on attacking the Union troops instead of moving to the defensive posture Longstreet continually suggests.

In Chapter 5, Longstreet begins to take a central role in the novel. By focusing on his character, Shaara advances the idea, once very popular among historians, that Longstreet was a visionary tactician who understood the nature of modern warfare before there really was such a thing. In an extended discussion with Fremantle, Longstreet explains how a single man with a rifle can kill at least three men on a battlefield, on average, when in a defensive posture—behind a tree, or in a trench. This view of Longstreet is partially based on Longstreet's own writings after the war, when it was very obvious that the Confederacy could have benefited from more defensive tactics. Shaara bases his characterization of Longstreet on a number of the man's own writings, so all the discussion of futuristic tactics and Longstreet's frustration at the backward or old-style strategies of Lee must be taken with a grain of salt. Longstreet became an advocate for defensive warfare after seeing it work well at Fredericksburg, but his enthusiasm was not necessarily based on a realization of the nature of modern warfare—he had seen defensive warfare work well, and so he thought it should be used more often.

JULY 1, 1863: CHAPTER 7

SUMMARY—CHAPTER 7: BUFORD
Late evening, Union camp. Buford returns to Cemetery Hill to survey the fortifications the Union army is building. Buford enters a farmhouse. Officers are arguing over who is really in command, General Howard or General Winfield Hancock. John Gibbon, one of Hancock's men, tells Buford that Howard is blaming Buford for the loss that day, claiming that Buford's men, who had fought all morning, should have supported Howard's men on the right flank. Hancock comes to talk to Buford, and Buford tells him about the death of Reynolds. Hancock orders Buford to get his cavalry refitted. General Meade arrives, and Buford leaves to brood.

ANALYSIS—JULY 1, 1863: CHAPTER 7
This small chapter essentially serves to cap Buford's role in the novel. For the rest of the book, the only Union officers on whom Shaara focuses are Chamberlain and his men. Buford returns, weary from the battle in the morning, only to discover he is the chosen scapegoat for the loss that day. This accusation is unfair, because Buford's brigades had seen so much action in the morning that they would not have been much help even if they had been able to attack from the right. Buford can theoretically shoulder some of the blame for the battle itself, because it is he who chose to occupy the hills in Gettysburg, which drew out General Heth's forces and led them to

attack the Union. Robert E. Lee had no intention of invading the town of Gettysburg. The two armies just stumbled into one another, and Buford made sure to choose the right ground—but in the process, he made a battle inevitable.

Lee is somewhat guilty of simply going with this idea. He wants to destroy the Union army in a single battle, and his attitude is that fate has picked Gettysburg as the place to do it. Longstreet thinks more broadly. He realizes that the time of the "one-battle war" is over, and his constant suggestion that the Confederate army should get between the Union army and Washington, D.C. comes from a very wide and long-term perspective on the war.

Buford has succeeded in securing the best high ground—Cemetery Hill, Cemetery Ridge, and Little Round Top—for the Union. The ground will once again be the focus of the battle the following day, when the Confederates concentrate their forces on the extreme right end of the Union army, Cemetery Hill and Culp's Hill, and the extreme left, Little Round Top. It is there, at Little Round Top, that the Union colonel, Joshua L. Chamberlain, takes his place in history in one of the most famous defenses of the Civil War.

July 2, 1863: Chapters 1–2

Summary—Chapter 1: Fremantle

Early morning, Confederate camp. English military observer Arthur Fremantle awakens, excited at the prospect of watching another battle—and, he hopes, another Confederate victory. He chats with other foreign observers, most notably a fat Austrian named Ross, and he marvels at how wonderful it is to be in the camp of what he thinks is the winning side. He rides to Gettysburg and climbs a tree to get a good view of the scene. He sees the officers meeting to discuss the plans for the day, and he wonders if there is any chance of the Confederacy rejoining England after the war. Lee arrives to meet with Longstreet, and Fremantle—conscious that the soldiers are laughing at him as he hangs in a tree—comes down. He speaks briefly with Ross, who is dressed in his bright blue, amusing war costume, complete with a metal helmet. Fremantle is quite unaware of the grave nature of the battle, and he always believes that the gentlemanly South will naturally win the war: "Fremantle knew with the certainty of youth and faith that [Longstreet] could not possibly lose this day, not with these troops, not with Englishmen, the gentlemen against the rabble." He is delighted, if a bit nervous, at the sound of the first cannon.

Fremantle asks Longstreet why the Confederates have not entrenched, wondering why they are not worried about a Union attack. Longstreet replies that Meade would never attack, and also that the Union forces are so fortified in their position that they would not want to move. Longstreet says, as he always does, that the best action for the Confederates is to swing around the Union army and come between them and Washington, D.C. to force the Union to attack. Of course, Lee will not agree to this plan.

Fremantle leaves to join his fellow Europeans. He muses again on how the "experiment" of America has failed, and the "equality of rabble" has changed back to a class system in just two generations— but only in the South. The South is "the Old Country." He believes he has stumbled on something profound.

SUMMARY — CHAPTER 2: CHAMBERLAIN

> *I was really thinking of killing him . . . and it was then*
> *I realized . . . I would kill them, and something at the*
> *same time said: you cannot be utterly right.*
> (See QUOTATIONS, p. 59)

Morning, Union camp just outside Gettysburg. Chamberlain sits with his regiment and awaits new orders. He cannot help thinking about his home in Maine, and his wife.

Private Kilrain comes over and informs Chamberlain that they have discovered an escaped slave. He is a large man who speaks little English, but he manages to thank the Union soldiers. Chamberlain has the surgeon bind the man's wounds and gives him food, but he cannot take the slave with the troops. He tries to point the slave in the right direction the best he can. Chamberlain is intrigued by the encounter—he has seen few black men in his life, and he finds himself somewhat bothered by his feelings when he sees the man. He feels slight revulsion, which occurs despite what he believes he should feel, and it irks him.

He begins to move the regiment forward. Another colonel appears and informs Chamberlain that his group is headed toward the small hill—Little Round Top.

Chamberlain again muses on the black man. He tells Kilrain that in his mind, there was never any real difference between black men and white men—black men have the same "divine spark" as other human beings. Kilrain says that while he has some reservations about blacks as a race, he thinks there are good ones and bad ones, just like white men. Chamberlain recalls an argument he had with a Southern preacher, who said that a Negro was not a man. Chamberlain left the room angrily. Another Southerner, a professor, came to him and apologized for the preacher's behavior, but he said he could not apologize for his views. He tried to persuade Chamberlain intelligently, as Chamberlain had tried to do with the preacher, and he had asked Chamberlain, "What if it is you who are wrong?" At that point Chamberlain found that he wanted to kill the Southern professor, despite his mild nature, and it was then that Chamberlain realized that this disagreement might come to war. Yet he also had his doubts. Kilrain calls Chamberlain an idealist.

ANALYSIS—JULY 2, 1863: CHAPTERS 1–2

Chapter 1 reasserts Fremantle's belief in the gentlemanly, English-like nature of the Confederacy. Fremantle, as a European, gives a perspective on Confederate culture from the outside. The Confederate forces are primarily white Anglo-Saxons, and the regular soldiers are mostly poor farmers and workers while the officers are all wealthy landowners. This class-based system also exists in England, and, consequently, Fremantle approves of it. He even hopes for a second that the Confederacy might rejoin the British Empire, which reveals just how misguided Fremantle's opinions are. Shaara makes Fremantle into a foppish, silly figure, but since Fremantle's part is based primarily on the book of memoirs the Englishman wrote just a few months after the battle, the characterization is probably one of the most accurate in the book.

Chapter 2 is the only chapter in the novel that deals with the issue of slavery. Shaara does not generally address the South's attitudes toward slavery, instead portraying the Confederate officers as fighting for "the Cause"—to protect their homeland and their way of life. There is little examination of the view that their way of life embodies racism and depends on slavery. The officers become indignant whenever slavery is brought up, and we never see nor hear the Confederates saying anything derogatory about blacks or slaves. Nor does Shaara try to paint the Northerners as noble comrades of African-Americans: Chamberlain, a Northerner, finds himself fighting feelings of revulsion when he meets an escaped slave who arrived recently from Africa. The slave is immensely muscled and he cannot speak English, and his traits give Chamberlain an unwelcome, animalistic impression of the black man.

The discussion between Chamberlain and Kilrain, and the treatment of the black man by the Union soldiers, is perhaps a bit unrealistic. While there are jokes about selling the slave back to the Confederacy, the Union soldiers are mostly kind to him. In fact, however, prejudice existed just as much in the North as in the South. But thoughtful, intelligent Chamberlain shows some of the attitudes Union soldiers had toward the men they were fighting to free. By 1863, many soldiers, especially those on the Union side, had forgotten the reasons for the war and knew only that they had to fight, day in and day out. They were becoming disillusioned by numerous losses at the hands of the Confederates. The scene with the slave helps remind us, as well as Chamberlain, of one of the reasons why the Union is fighting the Confederacy. But Chamberlain is also sufficiently contemplative about whether or not that freedom is worth the cost of so many lives.

JULY 2, 1863: CHAPTER 3

SUMMARY—CHAPTER 3: LONGSTREET

Morning, Confederate camp. Lee and Longstreet meet to discuss the plan of attack for that day. Longstreet still wants to fight defensively, but he realizes that Lee has made up his mind to attack that day. Ewell and Early think that the Union forces on Cemetery Hill and Culp's Hill are now too concentrated to attack. But they suggest that if Longstreet's men attack the left of the Union line, on Little Round Top and along Cemetery Ridge, they might draw off enough Union forces to allow Ewell and Early to take Cemetery Hill and Culp's Hill. Once Longstreet is heavily engaged with the enemy, Ewell's forces will strike.

Lee likes this plan, but he wants Longstreet's approval. The stubborn Longstreet refuses to give his approval, but he also refrains from arguing, so Lee simply orders him to attack the Union's left. Longstreet says that he must delay at least an hour until one more brigade arrives. Lee outlines his plan to General McLaws, who asks if he can send men to examine the roads leading to the Union's left before they march. Longstreet refuses, saying he does not want McLaws to leave his division. Another general, Hood, asks for permission to send a brigade around the end of the Union line to try to disrupt the supply lines in their rear. But Lee refuses the offer, saying he needs to concentrate his forces.

The officers leave to start the battle. Longstreet meets with Lee's engineer, Captain Johnston, who is to guide Longstreet's corps into position for the battle. Longstreet tells him to make sure the troops are not observed by Union soldiers. Johnston says he has scouted the Union position, but he has not scouted the roads leading up to it, and he fears that not knowing the roads will cause a problem. Longstreet grumbles to himself at the absence of Stuart, who would have reconnoitered all the roads around Gettysburg, had he been present.

The march begins at noon. Lee and Longstreet ride together, and for a moment they both feel somewhat giddy, almost looking forward to the assault. Then Longstreet reminds them that they once fought to defend the very people they are now attacking, making both men a bit depressed. Lee says that the "higher duty" was to Virginia, to their own people. Lee also talks about the difficulty of command, and of loving the army life but also knowing that he is constantly ordering his men to their deaths. Longstreet realizes that Lee thinks Longstreet is too close to the men and that Longstreet's love of defensive tactics comes from his unwillingness to order them to their deaths.

Lee rides off and Captain Johnson approaches. Johnson reports that if the troops march any farther on the road, the Union will be able to see them. Annoyed, Longstreet orders a countermarch that takes the troops almost to the point where they started and brings them around again, which costs a lot of valuable time. They discover that the Union troops have left Cemetery Ridge and dug in to the peach orchard just in front of Little Round Top. Longstreet is dismayed—Lee's orders will be difficult to carry out with the new Union position, but Longstreet cannot afford the time it would take to protest, and he doubts Lee would change his mind even if he could be reached. Hood objects to continuing the attack, since all their movements are observed, and the Union forces are already entrenched in the orchard. Since the Union troops have left the ridge, they have left their left flank unsupported and vulnerable. But Lee has ordered a frontal assault, and Longstreet believes he has no choice. Though the losses will be heavy, Longstreet orders Hood to attack the peach orchard. He tells Hood that he must take Little Round Top. The battle begins, and heavy losses occur quickly.

ANALYSIS—JULY 2, 1863: CHAPTER 3

Chapters 3 and 4 are the turning point of *The Killer Angels*. Both are long chapters that describe critical military actions on the Confederate side and the Union side. There are several instances here in which the Confederate army is not able to capitalize on the opportunities presented to them.

General Lee's insistence on a frontal assault creates significant problems for the Confederates, and it highlights the tension between his and Longstreet's views of the best strategies for conducting the war. Longstreet has been advising for days that the Confederacy should move southeast and come between the Union army and Washington, D.C. The Confederates would then find some good ground and dig in. The politicians in Washington would be terrified at the thought of having nothing between them and the Confederate army, and, therefore, they would force the Union general, Meade, to attack. This is the plan Longstreet has been pushing to Lee, but Lee does not want to fight defensively—he wants to win by show of force. Flush from two previous victories at Fredericksburg and Chancellorsville, Lee thinks he can finish the job at Gettysburg. Therefore Lee wants a frontal assault, and Longstreet, loyal to Lee, will not disobey orders, stubborn as he is. The situation becomes even more painful for Longstreet when he realizes that the Union army has actually come down off of Cemetery Ridge and occupied the peach orchard. With no troops on Little Round Top or Round Top, the Confederates could easily move southeast and attack from behind the Union position. But Longstreet is already late in his attack, and he orders Hood to attack the peach orchard from the front. This decision results in terrible losses on both sides, and it is one of the main factors leading to a Confederate defeat.

July 2, 1863: Chapter 4

Summary — Chapter 4: Chamberlain

> *Chamberlain raised his saber, let loose the shout that was the greatest sound he could make, boiling the yell up from his chest: Fix bayonets! Charge!*
>
> (See QUOTATIONS, p. 60)

Afternoon, south of Gettysburg. Chamberlain and his men are finally called upon to move, just as the Confederate attack begins. Chamberlain forms his regiment and waits for his orders. His commanding officer, Colonel Vincent, finally begins the march. As the men move forward, they begin to come within range of the artillery exchange. Chamberlain orders his brother Tom to move to the rear of the regiment, before it becomes "a hard day for mother." The regiment passes Big Round Top and begins to move up onto Little Round Top. Vincent places Chamberlain's regiment, the Twentieth Maine, on the southeastern side of Little Round Top. He tells Chamberlain, "You are the extreme left of the Union line. . . . The line runs from here all the way back to Gettysburg. But it stops here. . . . You cannot withdraw. Under any conditions. If you go, the line is flanked. . . . You must defend this place to the last."

Chamberlain's men immediately begin digging in, piling up rocks to build a stone wall. Chamberlain orders one of his men, Morrill, to take his company farther out to the left, in case the Confederates try to go around the Twentieth Maine and surprise them from the side. Chamberlain goes to the top of the hill and sees that the Union forces in the peach orchard are being overrun and that the Confederates will soon reach Little Round Top. He returns to his regiment. He tells the six prisoners from the former Second Maine that if they join the regiment now, there will be no charges. Three of the men take him up on the offer.

The infamous "Rebel yell" is heard, and the Confederate forces are on their way. Chamberlain finally realizes that he is the end of the Union line and that he has been ordered never to retreat.

The Confederates attack. The Twentieth Maine succeeds in repelling the initial charge. Chamberlain tries to reach Morrill to see if he and his company are all right, but a second attack quickly follows the first. This time, Kilrain is shot, but the wound seems slight, just under his armpit. Chamberlain jumps up on a rock and is promptly knocked down by a shot that lands near his foot. His foot hurts, but there is no hole in the boot. He climbs up on another boulder to get a better view and is shot again. This time the bullet glances off his sword scabbard.

Chamberlain calls all the commanders to him and orders them to hold the line. He says that they are about to be flanked on the left and that they have to stop the Confederates at all costs. He outlines a strategic maneuver, and the commanders quickly leave to execute his orders. Chamberlain returns to Kilrain, who is becoming weaker from his wound.

The Twentieth is beginning to run out of ammunition. The next attack hits hard all along the line. Chamberlain's men hold, but they are running very low on bullets. The next attack knocks a hole in the line, and Chamberlain instinctively orders the nearest man to fill it—his brother Tom. Tom survives the attack without injury.

The Twentieth Maine is now down to 200 men, having lost a hundred in the battle. The regiment does not have enough ammunition to handle another attack. Therefore, Chamberlain decides to order the men to fix their bayonets to their rifles and charge down the hill in a motion "like a swinging door" to sweep the Confederates away. Screaming, Chamberlain leads his men down the hill, and the plan works amazingly well, as the beleaguered Confederates flee in terror from the charging Union troops. As they try to escape, they run into Morrill's company. Many of the retreating Confederates are soon either dead, wounded, or taken prisoner.

Chamberlain returns to Kilrain, who has been shot in the arm again. Kilrain praises the job Chamberlain has done. Chamberlain meets up with Colonel Rice, the new brigade commander since Vincent was killed during the battle. Rice is very impressed with the bayonet charge.

The regiment has suffered casualties in nearly a third of its men. Kilrain is taken away to receive first aid, and Rice asks Chamberlain to move his men to Big Round Top. There will be no more fighting for them that day.

ANALYSIS — JULY 2, 1863: CHAPTER 4

The fight on Little Round Top is one of the most famous fights in the most famous battle of the Civil War. A single regiment, led by a professor-turned-colonel, is ordered to defend the extreme left flank of the Union army at all costs. They cannot retreat—if they do, the

Confederates will quickly come around behind the Union lines and attack from the rear. The chapter's central position in the book highlights the importance of the fighting at Little Round Top. The narrative also lionizes Chamberlain and his regiment. There are only two descriptions of combat in the book from observers actually in the midst of battle: Chamberlain at Little Round Top and, later, Lew Armistead during Pickett's Charge. Chamberlain's description is fast and action-oriented—it is likely that Shaara conceived much of the novel around the fighting at Little Round Top. The chapter moves at a breathless pace, culminating in the climactic bayonet charge. The chapter can almost serve as a short story by itself, with rising action, a climax, and falling action.

The narrator's description of Chamberlain's thoughts in sentence fragments gives us a sense of the quick-paced, confusing nature of combat: "He was knocked clean off the rock. Dirt and leaves in his mouth. Rolling over. This is ridiculous. Hands pulled him up." The swift action is broken up with scenes between Chamberlain and his men, particularly his brother Tom and Kilrain. These scenes give the chapter a plot beyond simply a recounting of historical details, and explain exactly what is going on between the sentence fragments: which soldiers are killed, what angle the Confederates attack from or are going to attack from, and how many bullets the Union soldiers have left. The breaks also give the characters a chance to reflect on the battle and give some meaning to it—Chamberlain's awareness of the fact that he cannot retreat under any circumstances lends psychological urgency to both the plot and his character.

The fact that both Tom and Chamberlain are fighting in the same regiment gives Shaara a way to reflect on the effect of war on family relationships. Tom's presence causes a great crisis for Chamberlain during the battle. Chamberlain realizes that the presence of a sibling "weakens a man" in combat when he hesitates to put his brother in a dangerous strategic position. He does so, but the action haunts Chamberlain for the rest of his life, and he writes about the experience in his memoirs of the war. Ultimately, Chamberlain decides to send his brother to another regiment, for two reasons: first, he cannot depend on himself to make the right decisions regarding Tom; and second, it is better to put distance between the two of them so that the odds of both of them dying at the same time are decreased.

JULY 2, 1863: CHAPTER 5–6

SUMMARY — CHAPTER 5: LONGSTREET

*Thing is, if anything bad happens now, they all blame it
on you. I seen it comin'. They can't blame General Lee.*
(See QUOTATIONS, p. 61)

Evening, Confederate camp. Longstreet moves through the make-
shift Confederate hospital, which is overflowing with wounded
from the day's battle. He sees General Hood, whose hand was
injured during the battle. The drugged Hood asks if the attack succeeded, and Longstreet lies and says it did. One of Longstreet's aides
tells him that Hood's officers are blaming Longstreet for the failure
of the attack. They would never blame Lee for a failed attack, so
they immediately turn to Longstreet. Longstreet's head aide, Sorrel,
reports that the casualties are heavy. Nearly half of the men in
Hood's division, 8,000 men, have been killed, wounded, or captured in two hours of fighting.

Longstreet thinks that there are no longer enough men for another
frontal assault and that Lee will therefore not order one the next day.
Longstreet orders Sorrel to get hard counts of the casualties and the
amount of ammunition and weapons remaining. As Sorrel rides
away, another aide appears to tell Longstreet that Pickett has finally
arrived. Longstreet tells the aide he will meet Pickett shortly.

Longstreet rides toward Lee's headquarters and finds Stuart
waiting outside, surrounded by reporters and admirers and enjoy-
ing the attention. Longstreet pays little attention. Longstreet meets
Lee, who draws him into the headquarters and away from the
press. Lee, thinking that the Union forces had nearly retreated, tells
Longstreet that he thought it was very close that day. Longstreet
thinks Lee is deluding himself. He tells Lee that there are three
Union corps dug into the high ground in front of him. Longstreet
pushes, one last time, for Lee to move the Confederate army
around to the right, to the southeast, and to put itself between the
Union army and Washington, D.C.

Another general appears and demands that Longstreet persuade
Lee to court-martial Stuart, who has left the Confederate army
blind to the Union's movements. Longstreet says he will talk to Lee,
but that he does not think it will do any good. Fremantle appears
and tries to congratulate Longstreet on his "victory." As they ride

along aimlessly, Longstreet realizes that Lee will attack the next day, an idea he thinks is suicidal. Fremantle claims that Lee is the most "devious" man he has ever met, and Longstreet replies that the Confederacy does not win with tactics, it wins with sheer determination. He is actually annoyed with the lack of tactics in the campaign, and thinks Lee does not use enough strategy. He says it will be a "bloody miracle" if the Confederates win the war. He resolves to speak to Lee in the morning, to make one last attempt to get him to move to the right.

Longstreet moves on and runs into Pickett and the other officers. Longstreet speaks with Armistead, who is disgusted by the fact that Fremantle thinks the Confederacy is fighting for slavery. Longstreet shrugs—he believes that the war is indeed about slavery, though that is not why he personally is fighting.

Armistead is old friends with Winfield Hancock, a Union general whom Longstreet fought earlier in the day. Armistead says that he had once vowed to Hancock that if he ever raised his hand against Hancock, then God may strike Armistead dead.

Eventually, the two men return to the party with the other officers, and forget their troubles for a few hours.

SUMMARY—CHAPTER 6: LEE

Late evening, Confederate camp. Lee considers his options for the following day. He recalls how he had once vowed to defend the very land he was attacking, when he was part of the whole United States army. Lee reflects on his past, and he tries to decide what to do. He considers a retreat, but realizes he has never seen men fight well after a retreat. He also knows his own army will never be stronger.

Stuart appears, having been sent for by Lee. Lee gently but firmly chastises the cavalry leader for joyriding and leaving him blind. Stuart tries to resign from his commission, but Lee will not accept his resignation and tells him to get back to work.

An aide reports to Lee that Ewell's camp is in much disorder because Ewell defers too much to Early. The aide tells Lee that Early and Ewell got the men moving very late, almost when Longstreet had finished his attack, thus ruining the plan to divide the Union's forces. It occurs to Lee that he has attacked the Union on both sides. The smartest next move, he thinks, would be to attack in the center. He decides to send his forces in to the center of Cemetery Ridge and break the Union army in two, then send Stuart and his cavalry around to the rear to finish the job.

ANALYSIS—JULY 2, 1863: CHAPTER 5–6

Chapter 5 again focuses on Longstreet, who has at this point become the protagonist of the novel. It is tragic that Longstreet is completely aware of how effective a defensive position would be, since it would likely have allowed his side to win the war. Shaara's characterization of Longstreet is at times enigmatic. While we see much of the Confederate perspective through him, he is a grim and quiet man, prone to responding to his fellow officers with single syllables, shrugs, and grunts. He has strong feelings about what the army should do, but he has been weakened by the death of his children and the knowledge that Lee has no intention of attempting his defensive strategies. Longstreet can see the defeat approaching, but he makes no move to stand up to Lee. He often agrees that Lee's plans could potentially work, though with heavy losses. His respect and admiration for Lee and for the chain of command is too strong for him to try and override Lee, and he knows Lee would ultimately censure him if necessary.

Shaara's characterization of Longstreet is probably overly sympathetic. In the second half of the nineteenth century, many Americans—soldiers and historians alike—began to blame Longstreet for the failure at Gettysburg, especially after Longstreet wrote a book blaming Lee. The book gave Longstreet a negative reputation all through the early twentieth century, until some historians began to see Longstreet in a more positive light—particularly in what they believed was his anticipation of modern warfare. Shaara perhaps portrays Longstreet as knowing more about how to correctly conduct the war than he actually did. Longstreet proposes the swing to the southeast over and over to Lee, who stubbornly refuses. In the true history, Longstreet was probably not so persistent in pushing for defensive tactics, and Lee was probably not so obtuse in his decision not to follow them.

JULY 3, 1863: CHAPTER 1–2

SUMMARY—CHAPTER 1: CHAMBERLAIN

Early morning, Big Round Top. From the hill's summit, Chamberlain watches the sun rise. Chamberlain's foot is still bleeding, and he has to keep moving to ignore the pain. His men are low on rations and hungry. Tom appears and offers Chamberlain some coffee. Chamberlain accepts it gratefully and remembers that he used his own brother to plug a hole in the front line the previous day. He misses Kilrain, who is absent because of his injury, and Chamberlain wishes he could talk to him. Tom reveals that he did not use his bayonet the previous day, as he could not bring himself to stab anyone. He points out that Chamberlain was never scared.

Chamberlain notices some artillery begin to fire in the north. He thinks they might be attacked again, but now the men have dug in deep and have plenty of ammunition. An aide arrives and says that Chamberlain's regiment has been relieved. The relief brigade quickly arrives, and the aide leads Chamberlain's men away and toward a "safe place" to rest, "right smack dab in the center of the line."

SUMMARY—CHAPTER 2: LONGSTREET

Morning, Confederate camp. Longstreet is preparing for the assault he knows is coming. There is still an opportunity to move southeast, but Union cavalry is quickly closing in on his army's flank. Lee arrives and the two ride out to survey the battlefield. Longstreet makes one last attempt to persuade Lee to move south, but Lee responds, "The enemy is there . . . and there's where I'm going to strike him." Lee wants Longstreet to move, with Pickett's fresh division in front, and split the Union line in the middle. Longstreet objects—he has lost half of his men, and one of his best officers, Hood, is injured. If he moves forward, the entire rear of the army is exposed. He informs Lee that it is his military opinion that a frontal assault will be a disaster.

But Lee is certain that the Union lines will break, and he sees no alternative. Before Longstreet can say anything, there is the sound of gunfire to the north. Apparently, Ewell has engaged the enemy without orders. But Lee and Longstreet soon discover that Union soldiers have actually attacked Ewell while he was getting ready, and their action surprises the Confederate officers. Ewell's battle begins to mount, and Lee makes his firm decision to charge the Union center. He tells Longstreet that he must reach a clump of trees on Cemetery Ridge. Longstreet replies, one last time, that he thinks the attack will fail, but Lee dismisses his concerns. Longstreet becomes despondent. He knows Lee will not relieve him and give the attack to someone else, because there is no one else capable of leading the charge. Yet he also knows that it is doomed to fail. Longstreet's depressed mood comes close to despair.

But Longstreet forces himself to move on, knowing that he cannot reveal his doubts to his officers. He orders the artillery commander, Alexander, to fire at the hill with as much ammunition as he has. Once Alexander thinks enough damage has been dealt, he is to let Longstreet know so the attack can begin.

Longstreet meets with his generals and describes the plan. They are all inspired and moved by the heroic plan, and they do not realize how hopeless it is. Longstreet is certain there will be terrible casualties. Longstreet knows there is nothing he can do but watch.

ANALYSIS—JULY 3, 1863: CHAPTER 1–2

In Chapter 1, Shaara makes his biggest departure from historical fact. He moves the Twentieth Maine from Big Round Top to a position in the center of the Union line, right where the Confederates attack the next day. But in fact, Chamberlain's regiment was moved to a ridge just north of Little Round Top, three quarters of a mile south of the line's center. Shaara makes this significant departure from history to show the Union perspective on Pickett's Charge. Moving Chamberlain also heightens the novel's drama by putting the Twentieth Maine once again in harm's way.

Chapter 2 focuses again on the struggle between Lee and Longstreet. It may seem frustrating that Longstreet, despite his vocal objections, never tries actively to prevent Lee from making the charge. Longstreet struggles with Lee in private, and when Lee proves obstinate, Longstreet backs down. Yet Longstreet does not seem like a weak-willed man—he is himself quite stubborn. One reason for the conflict may be that Shaara's allegiance to historical fact abbreviates his poetic license. Dramatically, it would make sense for Longstreet to persevere with Lee until Lee agreed, but since this is not actually what happened in the Civil War, Shaara's own rules about his novel's adherence to historical fact prevent him from portraying such an event. Longstreet follows Lee's orders in *The Killer Angels* because of his great respect for the man, and his knowledge that the Confederate troops think of Lee almost as a demigod. For Longstreet to go against Lee would be to make himself unpopular. Historically, however, Longstreet is responsible for his own share of personal mistakes in the battle. Furthermore, when Lee goes to see Longstreet on the morning of July 3, Longstreet is actually drawing up orders to move his men south and flank the Union right—he is ready take action despite Lee's opposition. Lee does not let Longstreet move the troops, and is also annoyed that Longstreet is unprepared to attack the Union's left flank, as Lee had originally planned. The plan, known as Pickett's Charge, was actually conceived then, in the morning. Shaara captures the gloominess of Longstreet that morning—he knew many men would die and that the plan would very likely fail.

July 3, 1863: Chapter 3–4

Summary—Chapter 3: Chamberlain

Chamberlain and his regiment march into the center of Cemetery Ridge. An aide tells Chamberlain that General Meade had wanted to retreat that morning, but the other generals had gathered together and forced him to remain, confident that the Confederates would attack again and that they could be repelled. General Hancock even predicts that the Confederates will attack the center of the line.

Chamberlain places his regiment, then heads over to the area where Meade and the other generals are having breakfast. He meets with his general, Sykes, who praises Chamberlain's actions the previous day on Little Round Top. Sykes hints that Chamberlain may become a brigade commander. Chamberlain returns to the area where the generals are and manages to get some chicken.

Chamberlain goes to rest and is joined by his brother Tom. Tom tells him that Kilrain has died. Suddenly, the Confederate artillery opens fire, and the world explodes around Chamberlain. He crawls around, trying to get out of the fire, and finally hides behind a stone wall, where he drifts in and out of sleep as the cannon shells land all around him. As the fire dies down an hour later, Chamberlain realizes an attack is coming and that he must form his regiment. But tired and weary from the blood loss of his foot wound, Chamberlain falls asleep again.

Summary—Chapter 4: Armistead

General Lew Armistead watches the Confederate guns fire upon the center of Cemetery Ridge. He sees General Pickett writing a letter to his young girlfriend. Armistead wanders around the lines, remembering his late wife and feeling gloomy. He knows that he will die soon. Armistead gives Pickett his wedding ring, and asks Pickett to send it to Armistead's girlfriend. After about an hour, the artillery fire subsides. The attack will soon begin. Armistead sees Dick Garnett, who has chosen to ride a horse into battle, though it is against orders. His foot is injured and, since he will be the only man riding a horse, he will be an easy target. Garnett realizes this risk, but he is riding to save his honor, and expects to die.

Armistead and Pickett ride into the woods to meet with Longstreet, who is gloomily sitting on his horse. Longstreet is crying. Then Longstreet gives the order for the charge, and Pickett rides away gleefully.

Armistead forms his brigade, and it begins to move toward the Union line. It is a steady, strong march, full of determination. Soon the Union artillery begins to open up, blowing huge holes in the Confederate lines. The Confederates repeatedly close up the holes, but soon the shells are falling all around them. Once they come close enough to the Union lines, the Union soldiers open up with musketry, riddling the front lines with bullets. Armistead sees Garnett's horse, without a rider. Screaming begins, and the lines begin to falter in their march. Soon the Confederates are fleeing, though some, like Armistead, continue to march and make it all the way to the clump of trees they were assigned to reach before they are shot. Armistead is shot, and he dies telling a soldier to send his regrets to his friend on the Union lines, General Hancock.

ANALYSIS—JULY 3, 1863: CHAPTER 3–4

Chapter 4 focuses on a character who has not previously had his own chapter, General Armistead. Armistead is one of the well-known figures in the battle, primarily due to his tragic friendship with Winfield Hancock of the Union army. Armistead and Hancock have metaphorically squared off in this battle, but Armistead simply misses his old friend. He never makes the trip over to speak to him, though he considers it several times throughout the novel. Their friendship highlights one of the more tragic aspects of the Civil War, since friends and even families were often pitted against each other in battle.

Historically, the Confederate losses during Pickett's Charge were staggering. The Confederates, well known to be fairly bad at artillery, overshot their targets, and few of the Union batteries were damaged. When the Confederates charged, the Union artillery simply mowed them down, and as the remaining Confederates approached the Union line they were killed by rifle fire. Pickett lost sixty percent of his men, and all thirteen of his colonels were either killed or wounded. Pickett emerged unscathed, but he was emotionally devastated and remained bitter toward Lee for the rest of his life.

The Battle of Gettysburg was as close as the South ever came to winning the war. If the army of the South had broken through the Union army and captured Washington, D.C., the war would have been over. With some better strategies on the Lee's part, it is possible that the South could have won the Battle of Gettysburg, which might have allowed it to win the war—but such speculation can be made about many Civil War battles. Nonetheless, Pickett's Charge was prefaced by the one of the largest artillery exchanges ever in the western hemisphere, and the battle itself was one of the largest ever between two armies. The Confederate army was at the height of its power and strength, but it could not break the Union's fortified position. The Confederate forces soon broke into a swift retreat.

July 3, 1863: Chapter 5–6

Summary—Chapter 5: Longstreet

Longstreet sits on a rail fence on Seminary Ridge, watching the horrific spectacle of Pickett's Charge unfold. Everything he has feared has come to pass. Men come screaming to him, asking for reinforcements, but he has already sent in every man he has. He orders Pickett to fall back. Fremantle, realizing the terrible loss the Confederacy has suffered, offers Longstreet a drink.

Longstreet knows the battle is over. He picks up a rifle and plans to walk down and join the last battery of guns still firing at the Union troops. Then he sees Lee riding among the troops, telling them the loss is "all his [Lee's] fault." The soldiers try to argue otherwise, but Lee knows he has failed. Pickett reappears, and Lee tells him to reform his division. In tears, Pickett replies that he has no division.

Longstreet mounts and rides toward the last battery, still firing uphill. His aides try to stop him, but he insists. He is soon joined by some of his staff. He rides forward until a shell knocks one of his aides off his horse. His aides pull him back and away from the rifle fire. The Union forces pull back and do not attack, though part of Longstreet wants them to come to his forces and end the war. Longstreet knows the Confederate army will never recover from this day.

Lee comes to Longstreet and tells him that they will withdraw that night to the river. Longstreet tells Lee that he does not think the war can be won now, and Lee does not disagree, though he does not agree either. He says, "If the war goes on—and it will, it will—what else can we do but go on? It is the same question forever, what else can we do? If they fight, we will fight with them. And does it matter after all who wins? Was that ever really the question? Will God ask that question, in the end?" The two generals ride off to oversee the retreat.

SUMMARY — CHAPTER 6: CHAMBERLAIN
Chamberlain rides out into the edges of the battlefield, still trying to clear the image of the approaching Confederates from his mind. He has seen Pickett's Charge, and he realizes that he has been a part of history. Tom comes to him, and admires the fight the Confederates put up. He expresses his amazement that the Confederates fight so hard for slavery. Chamberlain looks at all the dead men and says that they are all equal now, "in the sight of God."

Chamberlain remembers how he used his own brother to plug a hole in the regiment line, and he decides that he may have to send him away, as much as he would like to keep his brother nearby to watch him. However, he knows it will weaken his decisions to have a brother nearby.

A great storm breaks out, washing away much of the blood and bodies, and cleansing the land. Chamberlain and Tom return to their regiment prepared to continue fighting.

ANALYSIS — JULY 3, 1863: CHAPTER 5–6
The Confederate leaders, especially Longstreet, are quick to grasp the significance of the defeat. Lee, his confidence weakened by the loss, requests to be relieved of duty in August. Longstreet attempts to resign the following winter, claiming that he does not believe the South can win the war. Neither man is granted their request—the Confederate leaders will not let Lee resign, and Lee will not relieve Longstreet of duty. This knowledge may be part of what inspires the exchange between the two men in Chapter 5, in which both suspect that the war has just been lost, but they also know that they must continue to fight. Both men serve until the end of the war.

After Gettysburg, the battles on the eastern front of the war—between Lee's Army of Northern Virginia and the Union's Army of the Potomac—plodded slowly to a drawn-out, bloody Union victory almost two years later. Lee surrendered at Appomattox, and Chamberlain received the Confederate surrender. Chamberlain ordered his men to salute the surrendering soldiers as they marched by, a gesture of great respect.

Lee died in 1870 from heart disease. Longstreet spent the rest of his life an unpopular man after writing a memoir blaming Lee for the loss at Gettysburg, and for many years he was the target of biased historians, particularly those sympathetic to the Confederacy. Chamberlain went on to lead an impressive career: he served as governor of Maine for four years, and then as the president of Bowdoin College for twelve years. He was given a Congressional Medal of Honor in 1893 for gallantry at Gettysburg and wrote several books about the war. He died in 1914 at the age of eighty-three.

SUMMARY & ANALYSIS

Important Quotations Explained

1. Tell General Ewell the Federal troops are retreating in confusion. It is only necessary to push those people to get possession of those heights. Of course, I do not know his situation, and I do not want him to engage a superior force, but I do want him to take that hill, if he thinks practicable.

This passage is from July 1, Chapter 3. It is spoken by General Lee, and it is paraphrased from something the historical Lee said during the battle. Lee's statement is well known to historians, as it represents a small error that may have cost him a potential victory. The phrase "if he thinks practicable" allows Ewell to choose whether or not to attack Culp's Hill and Cemetery Hill. Many historians have argued that Lee's orders were never truly that ambiguous—Lee wanted the hills taken, unless the entire Union army was sitting on them. But Ewell, overly cautious, does not take the hills, and the Union army quickly digs into them. "Stonewall" Jackson had been killed several weeks before Gettysburg, and Ewell had been chosen to replace him. Many historians believe that Jackson, who knew how to move his troops, and who knew Lee very closely, would have taken the hills without hesitation.

2.   [A]wake all night in front of Fredericksburg. We
      attacked in the afternoon, just at dusk, and the stone
      wall was aflame from one end to the other, too much
      smoke, couldn't see, the attack failed, couldn't
      withdraw, lay there all night in the dark, in the cold
      among the wounded and dying. Piled-up bodies in
      front of you to catch the bullets, using the dead for a
      shield; remember the sound? Of bullets in dead
      bodies? . . . Remember the flap of a torn curtain in a
      blasted window, fragment-whispering in that awful
      breeze: never, forever, never, forever.

In this passage from July 1, Chapter 4, Chamberlain remembers the
Battle of Fredericksburg. The passage shows Chamberlain's impres-
sions of his early combat. Unlike many others fighting, Chamberlain was a citizen rather than a career soldier. These early battles and
the horror of piling up the corpses of his comrades to block bullets
have made a strong impression on his mind. But Chamberlain is an
intellectual who teaches in a college, so he remembers the horrors
imaginatively, possibly exaggerating their gravity in his mind.
Chamberlain's struggle to deal with the horrors of war illustrates
the difficulties that citizens-turned-soldiers had to face when they
entered the war.

QUOTATIONS

3.   I was really thinking of killing him, wiping him off the
      earth, and it was then I realized for the first time that
      if it was necessary to kill them, then I would kill them,
      and something at the same time said: you cannot be
      utterly right.

These lines are spoken by Chamberlain in July 2, Chapter 2. The
man he refers to is a fellow professor, from the South, who tries to
convince Chamberlain that blacks are not really "humans." Uncon-
vinced by Chamberlain's arguments, the professor asks Chamberlain, "What if it is you who are wrong?" Chamberlain is so enraged
at the man's racism that he wants to kill him, yet Chamberlain realizes that it is difficult to be so convinced of one's correctness as to
justify killing. The passage gives us the perspective of a Union intellectual on one of the causes of the war. Chamberlain has just met an
escaped slave—he has come face-to-face with what he knows is one
of the main reasons for the war. To his surprise, he finds himself
mildly repulsed by the sight of the slave, and his reaction troubles
him greatly. Many men on both sides felt that the war was being
fought over the issue of states' rights and the preservation of the
union rather than slavery. Chamberlain's deep contemplation of slavery and of his reaction to it, however, illustrates his understanding
that one of the fundamental causes of the war is indeed slavery.

4.   Chamberlain raised his saber, let loose the shout that
        was the greatest sound he could make, boiling the yell
        up from his chest: Fix bayonets! Charge! Fix
        bayonets! Charge! Fix bayonets! Charge! He leaped
        down from the boulder, still screaming, his voice
        beginning to crack and give, and all around him his
        men were roaring animal screams, and he saw the
        whole Regiment rising and pouring over the wall and
        beginning to bound down through the dark bushes,
        over the dead and dying and wounded. . . .

This passage is from July 2, Chapter 4. While *The Killer Angels* tells
the story of a terrible, real-life battle, it is at its heart an adventure
story, and there is no greater action scene in the novel than the
charge of the Twentieth Maine down Little Round Top. For over an
hour, the regiment has held off the Confederate soldiers attempting
to climb the hill. They have hidden behind trees and rock walls and
fired downward. But now they have run out of ammunition, and the
Confederates are still coming. They have been told they cannot
withdraw from the battle. Chamberlain sees only one chance: to
charge down the hill, bayonets and swords aloft, and try to get the
Confederates to flee. The plan works perfectly: the Confederates
flee in terror from the screaming Union soldiers. It is a powerful
moment, and this scene is also the centerpiece of the film *Gettysburg*. The novel and film have made the fighting on Little Round
Top almost as famous as the Battle of Gettysburg itself.

5.   Thing is, if anything bad happens now, they all blame it on you. I seen it comin'. They can't blame General Lee. Not no more. So they all take it out on you. You got to watch yourself, General. . . . I saw you take all morning trying to get General Lee to move to the right.

This passage is spoken by Goree, an aide to Longstreet, in July 2, Chapter 5. It foreshadows the fact that Longstreet will eventually be blamed for the loss at Gettysburg. Longstreet's memoir, which attacks Lee for not moving to the right at Gettysburg, inspires much of this blame. Longstreet soils the memory of one of the most beloved figures in Southern history, and his fellow Southerners scorn him for the rest of his life. Many soldiers in their memoirs refer to Pickett's Charge as "Longstreet's Charge." For decades, Longstreet does indeed take an unfair amount of blame for the loss at Gettysburg. Even after twentieth-century scholars constructed a less biased view of the battle, Longstreet is still a more obscure general than Lee.

Key Facts

FULL TITLE
The Killer Angels

AUTHOR
Michael Shaara

TYPE OF WORK
Novel

GENRE
Historical fiction; Civil War fiction

LANGUAGE
American English

TIME AND PLACE WRITTEN
Late 1960s and early 1970s, United States

DATE OF FIRST PUBLICATION
1974

PUBLISHER
David McKay

NARRATOR
Anonymous

POINT OF VIEW
The narrator usually sticks to a third-person, omniscient form of narration. It is the subjective form, meaning that the focus is primarily on the central character of that chapter, whoever it may be. If we enter a character's thoughts, they are almost always the thoughts of that central character.

TONE
The novel is written in a very epic tone. The historical setting and the dramatic use of real—and very famous—historical characters sets it apart from most historical fiction.

TENSE
Immediate past, or real-time narration

SETTING (TIME)
June 30–July 3, 1863

SETTING (PLACE)
Gettysburg, Pennsylvania, a small farm town surrounded by a few hills and ridges: Seminary Ridge, which the Confederates control; and Cemetery Hill, Cemetery Ridge, Culp's Hill, Little Round Top, and Big Round Top, all controlled by the Union.

PROTAGONIST
General Robert E. Lee; General James Longstreet; Colonel Joshua L. Chamberlain

MAJOR CONFLICT
The Confederate States fight a war against the Union to establish their right to secede.

RISING ACTION
The Confederate States fail to capture the high ground in the hills around Gettysburg, allowing the Union army to take a strategic, defensive position.

CLIMAX
The climax of the novel might seem to be Pickett's Charge, when the Confederates soldiers make one incredibly brave, yet utterly futile march across a field into enemy artillery. Also, some may place the climax at Chamberlain's decision to have his officers charge at the enemy in utter desperation with bayonets instead of ammunition. Yet another interpretation might place the climax at the scene where General Lee makes his final refusal to follow General Longstreet's advice to swing southeast toward Washington, D.C. and fight defensively instead. Longstreet knows that Pickett's Charge will fail, and once Lee has chosen to make the charge, the Confederates' bloody loss becomes inevitable.

FALLING ACTION
Pickett's Charge ends in heavy losses for the Confederacy. Lee puts the Confederate army into retreat, while Chamberlain muses on the amazing sight of Pickett's Charge earlier in the day. Longstreet and Lee know that the war will not end, but both of them suspect that the Confederacy has just lost.

KEY FACTS

THEMES
: Technology and strategic development; the obtrusiveness of death in war; a nation divided

MOTIFS
: Loyalty, command errors, aristocracy

SYMBOLS
: Lee's heart trouble

FORESHADOWING
: Longstreet's constant pushing for a defensive posture and Lee's equally firm refusals imply that Lee is going to make a wrong move somewhere, and he does so with Pickett's Charge.

KEY FACTS

Study Questions & Essay Topics

Study Questions

1. *One of the major conflicts in the novel is the disagreement between Confederate generals Robert E. Lee and James Longstreet on how they should fight the battle. What does each man think the army should do and why? What is significant about Longstreet's plan?*

The most overt conflict in *The Killer Angels,* aside from the battle itself, is the argument between Lee and Longstreet over whether to use offensive or defensive tactics. Longstreet has come to understand the modern nature of warfare: he realizes that new technology, such as long-range artillery and repeating, breech-loading rifles, means the old strategies of war can no longer work as well. A single man armed with a good rifle and in a defensive position— behind a tree, for instance—can kill at least three men charging toward him from across a field, says Longstreet. That means that 1,000 men can kill 3,000 charging across the same field. Longstreet argues that even more men can be killed if the defender is aided by artillery. Longstreet believes that fortified, defensive positions are the best way to win a battle, and so he suggests that Lee move the Confederate army to a position southeast of Gettysburg, so the Confederates come between the Union army and the Union capital, Washington, D.C. This strategy will force the Union army to attack to protect the capital, and if the Confederates dig in to a defensive position, they can simply destroy the Union army as it attacks. Longstreet's strategy is remarkably modern in theory, and Shaara portrays Longstreet as a man who is ahead of his time.

Robert E. Lee, however, is a more traditional soldier, and he believes he can destroy the Union army—even in a fortified, high ground position—if he simply puts his men in the right places. After two days of battering the right and left flanks of the Union army, he finally tries to break through the center with Pickett's Charge. He believes this tactic will allow him to cut the Union army in two and then destroy the confused pieces that remain. But Lee underestimates the Union artillery, secured in the high ground of Cemetery Ridge, which utterly demolishes the Confederate soldiers as they attempt to cross the field. Pickett's Charge was the last great infantry charge—never again would so many men slowly march across a field to strike their enemies. Advancements in artillery and rifle technology ended the age of such strategies, and Pickett's Charge, whether or not a wise plan, marked the end of this era.

2.   *Why did the Confederate army lose the Battle of Gettysburg?*

In *The Killer Angels*, General John Buford, the Union cavalry commander, is quick to seize the high ground. Specifically, he tries to protect Seminary Ridge and the hills behind it: Cemetery Hill, Cemetery Ridge, Culp's Hill, Little Round Top, and Big Round Top. The Union yields Seminary Ridge, but manages to hold on to the rest of the hills. These hills are excellent defensive positions: they allow officers to see much of the surrounding area, they are covered with rocks and trees that can block bullets, and artillery has a greater range when fired from high positions. Robert E. Lee is annoyed with General Ewell for not seizing Culp's Hill or Cemetery Hill. Chamberlain's regiment defends Little Round Top, having been ordered never to retreat. The high ground is one of the major elements of the Union victory.

Furthermore, without J. E. B. Stuart, Lee has no information about the movements of the Union army or the geography of the surrounding area. As a result, strategic planning is very difficult for Lee, particularly since he is in unfamiliar, Northern territory. First, Pickett's Charge—Lee's attempt to completely destroy the Union army—fails, since the Confederate artillery attack prior to the charge misses most of its targets, leaving the Union with almost all its batteries. Second, Lee vastly underestimates the power of the Union position. The Union artillery mows down the advancing Confederate soldiers, killing or wounding nearly sixty percent of them.

3. *The main characters on the Confederate side are all generals: Robert E. Lee, James Longstreet, George Pickett, and Lew Armistead. But the main character on the Union side is a colonel, Joshua L. Chamberlain. Why would the author choose to use Chamberlain instead of the Union generals?*

There are numerous reasons why Shaara might choose to focus on Chamberlain. Part of Shaara's decision may be a lack of action on the part of the Union generals. They spend most of their time directing defensive maneuvers, which are perhaps less interesting than Lee's plans to attack the Union flanks. The Union commander, George Meade, does not even arrive until the night of July 1. Furthermore, Meade does not have a fraction of the reputation of other Union generals like Ulysses S. Grant, or even John Hooker or George McClellan, and he certainly cannot compare to Robert E. Lee, whose reputation overshadows almost all other Civil War figures except Grant. Another interesting general, Reynolds, is killed just as the battle begins, cutting off another potential character. Lee and Longstreet grow to be legends in their own time, and each becomes even more famous in the nostalgic fervor that eventually surrounds the Civil War. Meade, on the other hand, develops a reputation, probably unfairly, of being a rather poor general who got lucky at Gettysburg, and was eventually replaced by Grant. The Union also lacks flamboyant characters like Pickett. This does not mean that Shaara would not have been able to write a good story from the perspective of the Union generals—it just explains, partially, why he may not have chosen to do so.

Shaara's focus on Joshua L. Chamberlain is much easier to explain. Chamberlain was never an obscure figure to Civil War historians. After the Battle of Little Round Top, Chamberlain became even more famous for receiving the surrender of the Confederate forces at Appomattox. There, he ordered his men to salute their vanquished foes. He later served as the governor of Maine and the president of Bowdoin College, and received a Congressional Medal of Honor for his bravery at Little Round Top. Finally, Chamberlain wrote a series of memoirs on his experiences during the war, giving even more information about the now-legendary Battle of Little Round Top. Chamberlain was a college professor who left his job in order to serve his country. He represents the ideal citizen-soldier, an intellectual who voluntarily leaves his comfortable civilian life to become an excellent soldier. The fact that Chamberlain is well educated allows Shaara to examine the thoughts and motivations of the Union soldiers during the war.

SUGGESTED ESSAY TOPICS

1. Is Longstreet wrong to obey Lee's orders, even though he disagrees? Should he have tried to get the other generals to help him change Lee's mind? Why doesn't Longstreet try to take command from Lee?

2. Why is Chamberlain so bothered about having his brother serving with him in his regiment? Why would he want to order his brother out of the regiment?

3. Author Michael Shaara changes some of the historical facts about the battle—for instance, he puts Chamberlain in the middle of the Union line during Pickett's Charge, when in fact Chamberlain was more than a mile south at the time. Why do you think Shaara does this? Do you think it is good or bad to change the facts in a historical novel?

4. Discuss how the issue of slavery is dealt with by the characters in *The Killer Angels*. Be sure to cite examples from both Confederate and Union characters.

5. Discuss death and the way it is dealt with by the characters in *The Killer Angels*.

Review & Resources

Quiz

1. From where is Joshua L. Chamberlain?

   A. Georgia
   B. Virginia
   C. New Hampshire
   D. Maine

2. Who tells Longstreet that the Union army is very close by?

   A. General Lee
   B. Harrison
   C. Sorrel
   D. General J. E. B. Stuart

3. What part of General Lee causes him pain?

   A. His knee
   B. His heart
   C. His arm
   D. His toe

4. Who leads the Union cavalry?

   A. General John Reynolds
   B. General J. E. B. Stuart
   C. General John Buford
   D. Sorrel

5. Which of the following is not a battle site?

   A. Follicle Hill
   B. Cemetery Ridge
   C. Little Round Top
   D. Big Round Top

6. Which general leads the Union forces at Gettysburg?

    A.   Robert E. Lee
    B.   George C. Meade
    C.   Ulysses S. Grant
    D.   Arthur Fremantle

7. Which Union officer is killed just as the battle begins?

    A.   Buford
    B.   Chamberlain
    C.   Reynolds
    D.   Kilrain

8. Which Confederate general fails in his assignment of monitoring the movements of the Union army?

    A.   Stuart
    B.   Ewell
    C.   Armistead
    D.   Longstreet

9. How long did the Battle of Gettysburg last?

    A.   One week
    B.   Three days
    C.   Five days
    D.   One day

10. Which famous general of the Confederate army was killed a few weeks before the Battle of Gettysburg?

    A.   "Stonewall" Jackson
    B.   J. E. B. Stuart
    C.   James Longstreet
    D.   Jubal Early

11. What physical ailment bothers General Lee during the battle?

    A.   Headaches
    B.   A stiff leg
    C.   Heart problems
    D.   Backache

12. Which Confederate general did not survive the Battle of Gettysburg?

   A.   J. E. B. Stuart
   B.   James Longstreet
   C.   George Pickett
   D.   Lew Armistead

13. Which soldier has a brother under his own command?

   A.   Joshua L. Chamberlain
   B.   Robert E. Lee
   C.   James Longstreet
   D.   George Pickett

14. What is the capital of the Confederacy?

   A.   Richmond
   B.   Washington, D.C.
   C.   Gettysburg
   D.   St. Louis

15. What is the real name of the Confederate army?

   A.   Lee's Lawmen
   B.   The Army of Northern Virginia
   C.   The Rough Riders
   D.   The Army of the Potomac

16. Which ally of Chamberlain is shot during the Battle of Little Round Top?

   A.   Tom Chamberlain
   B.   Winfield Hancock
   C.   John Hood
   D.   Buster Kilrain

17. What job did Joshua L. Chamberlain hold before the war?

   A.   He was a farmer
   B.   He was an insurance salesman
   C.   He was a blacksmith
   D.   He was a college professor

REVIEW & RESOURCES

18. What type of military strategy does James Longstreet endorse?

     A. Pickett's Charge
     B. He wants to attack the Union on both flanks
     C. He wants to swing around behind the Union army and block them off from Washington, D.C.
     D. He wants to attack in the middle of the night and surprise the Union forces

19. Union general Winfield Hancock is friends with which Confederate general?

     A. James Longstreet
     B. George Pickett
     C. Lew Armistead
     D. John Hood

20. What is the name of Chamberlain's regiment?

     A. The Third Maine
     B. The Forty-Fourth New York
     C. The Twentieth Maine
     D. The Forty-Ninth San Francisco

21. In what state is Gettysburg?

     A. Virginia
     B. West Virginia
     C. North Carolina
     D. Pennsylvania

22. What high ground does Chamberlain's regiment have to protect?

     A. Culp's Hill
     B. Little Round Top
     C. Seminary Ridge
     D. Cemetery Hill

23. What is cavalry?

    A. Soldiers who fight on foot
    B. Soldiers who fight on horses
    C. Soldiers who build bridges to cross rivers
    D. Men who entertain the troops

24. What is the name of the Englishman observing the Confederate army?

    A. Arthur Fremantle
    B. Ichabod Crane
    C. Sorrel
    D. Taylor

25. Pickett's Charge was not actually planned by Pickett. Whose idea was the charge?

    A. General John Reynolds
    B. General James Longstreet
    C. General Lew Armistead
    D. General Robert E. Lee

REVIEW & RESOURCES

ANSWER KEY:
1: D; 2: B; 3: B; 4: C; 5: A; 6: B; 7: C; 8: A; 9: B; 10: A; 11:
C; 12: D; 13: A; 14: A; 15: B; 16: D; 17: D; 18: C; 19: C; 20:
C; 21: D; 22: B; 23: B; 24: A; 25: D

SUGGESTIONS FOR FURTHER READING

CHAMBERLAIN, JOSHUA L. *Bayonet Forward: My Civil War Reminiscences.* Gettysburg, Pennsylvania: S. Clarke Military Books, 1994.

CODDINGTON, EDWIN B. *The Gettysburg Campaign: A Study in Command.* New York: Scribners, 1968.

HARTWIG, D. SCOTT. *A* KILLER ANGELS *Companion.* Gettysburg, Pennsylvania: Thomas Publications, 1996.

LONGSTREET, JAMES. *From Manassas to Appomattox : Memoirs of the Civil War in America.* Philadelphia: J.B. Lippincott Co., 1896.

MCPHERSON, JAMES M. *Battle Cry of Freedom: The Civil War Era.* New York: Oxford University Press, 1988.

PFANZ, HARRY. *Gettysburg: The First Day.* Chapel Hill, North Carolina: University of North Carolina Press, 2001.

SYMONDS, CRAIG L., ED. *American Heritage History of the Battle of Gettysburg.* New York: HarperCollins, 2001.

REVIEW & RESOURCES

A Note on the Type

The typeface used in SparkNotes study guides is Sabon, created by master typographer Jan Tschichold in 1964. Tschichold revolutionized the field of graphic design twice: first with his use of asymmetrical layouts and sanserif type in the 1930s when he was affiliated with the Bauhaus, then by abandoning assymetry and calling for a return to the classic ideals of design. Sabon, his only extant typeface, is emblematic of his latter program: Tschichold's design is a recreation of the types made by Claude Garamond, the great French typographer of the Renaissance, and his contemporary Robert Granjon. Fittingly, it is named for Garamond's apprentice, Jacques Sabon.

SPARKNOTES TEST PREPARATION GUIDES

The SparkNotes team figured it was time to cut standardized tests down to size. We've studied the tests for you, so that SparkNotes test prep guides are:

Smarter:
Packed with critical-thinking skills and test-
taking strategies that will improve your score.

Better:
Fully up to date, covering all new features of the tests,
with study tips on every type of question.

Faster:
Our books cover exactly what you need to
know for the test. No more, no less.

SparkNotes Guide to the SAT & PSAT
SparkNotes Guide to the SAT & PSAT — Deluxe Internet Edition
SparkNotes Guide to the ACT
SparkNotes Guide to the ACT — Deluxe Internet Edition
SparkNotes Guide to the SAT II Writing
SparkNotes Guide to the SAT II U.S. History
SparkNotes Guide to the SAT II Math Ic
SparkNotes Guide to the SAT II Math IIc
SparkNotes Guide to the SAT II Biology
SparkNotes Guide to the SAT II Physics

SparkNotes Study Guides: